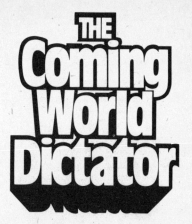

THE Coming World Dictator

John Wesley White

Bethany Fellowship INC.
MINNEAPOLIS, MINNESOTA 55438

All Scripture quotations are taken from the
King James Version of the Bible

The Coming World Dictator
John Wesley White

Library of Congress Catalog Card Number 80-71003

ISBN 0-87123-042-9

Published by Bethany Fellowship, Inc.
6820 Auto Club Road, Minneapolis, Minnesota 55438

Printed in the United States of America

About the Author

JOHN WESLEY WHITE is an associate evangelist of the Billy Graham Evangelistic Association. Born in Canada, he now resides in Toronto. He was educated in five countries, culminating in the earning of a Doctor of Philosophy degree from Oxford University in England. Since joining the Billy Graham organization, he has been to a hundred countries in every part of the world. He has preached to crowds as large as 35,000 and has seen over 100,000 come forward to make decisions for Christ. Chancellor of Richmond College in Toronto, he is, in addition, speaker on the coast-to-coast TV program "Agape," on which, with George Beverly Shea and others, he has shared the Gospel of Christ with additional millions.

Other Books by the Same Author:

The Man from Krypton
What Does It Mean to Be Born Again?

Foreword

St. John, who makes several allusions to the Antichrist, states that in "the last time . . . antichrist shall come" (1 John 2:18). Through Daniel we're introduced to a personage who acquires power—wicked, wonder-working power, very much like the character to whom Paul refers in the second chapter of 2 Thessalonians.

The world today is everywhere looking for a superman. A governor, scanning the potential candidates, mused, "I am looking for a messiah, and no one measures up." Sober-minded Cambridge historian, the late Arnold Toynbee, reckoned that man in his present plight is "ripe for the deifying of any new Caesar who might succeed in giving the world unity and peace."

Every Christian should be committed to peace. The Scriptures exhort us to pray for peace, seek peace, pursue peace, hope for peace. Jesus assured, "Blessed are the peacemakers." So as another New Year rings in to the sound of the peace bell, we are to join the effort to promote worldwide peace.

On the other hand, Jesus made clear that before His second coming there would come pretenders saying, "I am Christ. . . . And ye shall hear of wars and rumors of wars." The siren warnings of an impending Armageddon are much more evident in the world today than the ringing of peace bells.

John Wesley White, one of my associate evangelists since 1964, has been of invaluable assistance to me in the area of research. During his time with me, he has traveled to a hundred countries, preaching the gospel. In a crusade held in Sioux Falls, South Dakota, he witnessed 2,000 inquirers coming forward to make decisions for Christ. He has also carried on a weekly coast-to-coast television ministry for seven years. He is a compassionate and compellingly persuasive evangelist.

When someone reads this sobering—and at times frightening—book, he should note one imperative point: even more important than an examination of the prophecies concerning the coming of the Antichrist is *the proclamation of the second coming of Christ*. No Gospel theme, apart from "Ye must be born again," is more relevant today; I preach on some facet of this subject in virtually all of my crusades. It behooves the people of the whole world to do as the ancient prophet Amos urged, "Prepare to meet thy God!"

Billy Graham
Montreat, N.C.
January, 1981

Preface

Some people argue that in this scientifically oriented era, no mere man could rise up as an antichrist and seize the reins of world government. I suggest that they consider the precedent set by John Lennon, whose tragic death just happens to be world headlines at the time I take up my pen and write this Preface.

Lennon was the founder and philosophical force behind the Beatles. A *Toronto Star* editorial, in the wake of 35,000 devotees who marched downtown with candles to memorialize him, reckoned that Lennon was, more than any other single individual, the prime mover behind the mindset and mood of our generation. Harvard hippie guru, Dr. Timothy Leary, said, "John was the unwitting leader" of the "worldwide revolutionary change" which characterizes our times. John Lennon was, in the social arena, what Vladimir Lenin was in the political arena during a previous generation.

Jerry Rubin stated, "John Lennon was the one individual who had the most profound effect on my generation," adding, "We took [Lennon] to the streets. That was the Yippie movement—burning money on Wall Street and running a pig for president. It was the guerilla theater of the soul."

John Baldry recalls, "By 1964 the whole world had fallen in love with John Lennon." And so totally had he enshrined himself in the hearts of his tens of millions of followers that Bob Segar eulogized, "I can imagine a world without nations, a world of peace, but I cannot imagine a world without John Lennon."

Just what relevance has all this to the coming Antichrist? Derek Taylor, the Beatles' press agent during their peak years, assessed they were "absolutely rude, profane, vulgar"; they were "*completely antichrist.* . . . I am antichrist, but these boys even shock me."

Lennon became notorious for his statement, "Christianity will go. It will vanish and shrink. I needn't argue about that; I'm right and I will be proved right. We're more popular than Jesus now."

Lennon is gone. But Antichrist is yet to come! "Antichrist shall come," but so will Jesus Christ. The time will arrive when "at the name of Jesus every knee should bow, of things in heaven, and things in earth, and things under the earth; and that every tongue should confess that Jesus Christ is Lord, to the glory of God the Father" (Phil. 2:10, 11).

John Wesley White, D.Phil.
Toronto, Canada
January, 1981

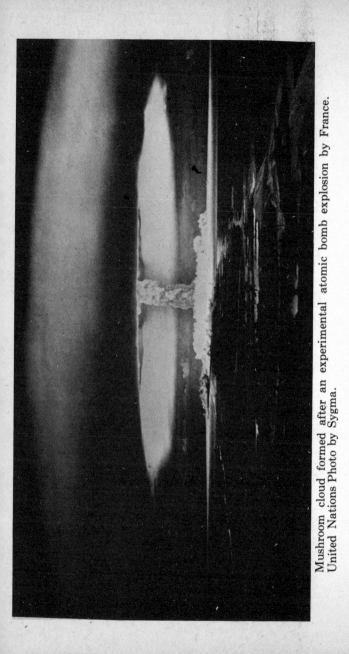

Mushroom cloud formed after an experimental atomic bomb explosion by France. United Nations Photo by Sygma.

Chapter One

"Make it plain" (Hab. 2:2).

The world has always felt it ought to be warned about the perils of impending economic, ecological, or nuclear disaster which endanger it. But the use of Bible prophecy for such purposes has not been considered "chic" in scholarly circles; rather, it has been discounted as "sensationalism."

As the world situation draws increasingly closer to the brink of catastrophe, popular cynicism toward Bible prophecy has begun to crumble as leaders grope to comment on the future. For instance, Pope John Paul II recently lamented, "We can instinctively apply to our times the words of the prophet Isaiah [60:2]: 'Darkness will cover the earth; fog will smother the nations.' "

In late 1980, CBS broadcast a four-hour special depicting war and woe at their barbaric worst; it was entitled, "Rumor of War." This, of course, was borrowed from Jesus' promise that "ye shall hear of wars and rumours of wars" (Matt. 24:6).

Dr. Ernest Howse, former Moderator of the United Church of Canada and prominent liberal clergyman, recently astonished many with a statement in his weekly syndicated column. He joined the Jeremiahs of history by stating that a look into the future reveals "the world is dark with what seems like the sunset of civilization." He continued, "Prophecies of global disaster, which before would have been dismissed as lunatic, are now seriously spoken, and everywhere stun the mind with terrifying dreams and incomprehensible dread." People facing "an intolerable fate are rushing blindly to a crossroads encounter with doom."

Perhaps these public referrals to Scripture as an answer to the present conditions will have an effect on society's view toward Bible prophecy.

Certainly there's no comfort in turning to the secular leaders of our time. Elevated to leadership of the People's Republic of China, the most populous nation in history, Chairman Deng Xiaoping emphasizes his belief that "a third world war is inevitable," and that he is "convinced that the war will break out in the 1980s." Curiously, despite his professed atheism, Deng is sure that the war will be "independent of man's will." Such a statement brings him full circle through Darwinism, Marxism, and almost back to Calvinism!

Now in his second term as President of France, Valery Giscard D'Estaing concludes that "the world is unhappy. It is unhappy because it doesn't know where it is going and because it senses that if it knew, it would discover it was heading for disaster."

Perhaps the most frightening bestseller to appear on the bookstands in the last few years is Isaac Asimov's *A Choice of Catastrophies*. In it, Asimov presents various horrible ways that man, as he exploits nature, is preparing to destroy himself. The problem an intelligent reader faces is that Asimov is so convincing.

When Walter Cronkite commented on Alvin Toffler's recent bestseller, *The Third Wave*, he predicted that we are headed for either a new Renaissance or a new Dark Age, the evidence weighing heavily toward the latter.

The late Marshall McLuhan, foremost intellectual in Canada, warned that we must attempt to steer mankind clear of a nuclear war that would almost certainly annihilate all life on this planet.

With a note of despair, Marshall Shulman, a Carter Administration expert on the Soviet Union, said in late 1980, "Sometimes I get the feeling I'm sitting on a hilltop watching two trains racing toward each other on the same track."

In Toronto, during the summer of 1980, the First Global Conference on the Future, organized by the World Future Society, was intended to be "the most prestigious, representative and definitive conference on the future ever to be held on this planet." (A rather audacious purpose, in the light of the fact that Jesus, the Son of God, spoke on this theme almost 2,000 years ago.) However, no positive ideas arose at this conference to ensure a future for man. Rather, the emphasis was one of doom, exemplified by Canada's Governor-General Ed Shrier, who proposed that unless man could find a prompt solution to his nuclear dilemma, he had no future at all.

For those who prefer to approach the chances of human survival from a gambler's standpoint, pundit Dick Beddoes insists that he knows of no serious oddsmaker who would give man more than an 8-to-5 chance of surviving into the twenty-first century. In the past such outlooks were supposed to be the special preserve of the Bible wielders.

Jesus warned that the times of the Antichrist will be the worst the world has ever known. In His discourse to the disciples regarding "the tribulation of those days," as recorded in Matthew 24, Mark 13, Luke 21, and John 16, He foretold a period of false messiahs, rumors of war, sorrow, betrayal, deceit, iniquity, persecution and catastrophe. Conditions will be so horrible that "except those days should be shortened, there should no flesh be saved" (Matt. 24:22).

But there is marvelous hope! Jesus affirmed

plainly that these holocaustic horrors would not be death pains, but birth pangs; that His coming would be like the birth of a child, after which a mother, despite the suffering she has undergone, rejoices that her baby is born. There really is a "new world coming," though not something which man or the Antichrist develops; it will be the Kingdom which Jesus Christ inaugurates in His second coming.

We need not have any apprehensions. Though the Scriptures are filled with warnings, they are also filled with hope. Only in the Bible can we find a reaffirmation of man's future. Twenty-five centuries ago, God spoke to His prophet Habakkuk about the second coming of Christ (this was 600 years before Christ's *first* appearance). Habakkuk wrote:

> I will stand upon my watch, and set me upon the tower, and will watch to see what he will say unto me. . . . And the Lord answered me, and said, Write the vision, and make it plain upon tables, that he may run that readeth it. For the vision is yet for an appointed time, but at the end it shall speak, and not lie: though it tarry, wait for it; because it will surely come, it will not tarry. (Hab. 2:1-3)

The writer to the Hebrews shows that the above passage refers to Christ's *second* coming when he quotes part of it: "For ye have need of patience, that, after ye have done the will of God, ye might receive the promise. For yet a very little while, and he that shall come will come, and will not tarry" (Heb. 10:36, 37).

When dealing with the events surrounding Christ's return, we must "make it plain." This was the Apostle Paul's desire as he wrote the Thessalonians concerning the coming of "the man of sin" and the coming of Christ. He emphasized to these brethren that "I would not have you to be ignorant" (1 Thess. 4:13) in these matters. And that is the exact purpose of this book, as well.

Chapter Two

"Antichrist shall come" (1 John 2:18).

We exist in a "leaderless world" was Walter Cronkite's recent verdict—not a comforting one!

Reinhold Kerstan, author of *Blood and Honor*, where he reflects on his boyhood in Hitler's Germany, concludes that North Americans are desperately seeking for "the leader" who will "point the way out of economic decline and uncertainty. A generation deprived of any teaching of moral absolutes is wide open to an updated Fuehrer."

Journalist and ardent Kennedy supporter, Haynes Johnson, was being interviewed on national television after his desired candidate had been defeated in the presidential primaries. He lamented that though he was "not a theologian," he supposed that Americans are "expecting a godlike figure as President." He then asked, "Do we have such a man?"

The Scriptures assure that this man's question will be answered, that "antichrist shall come"—not merely as a candidate for President of the United States, but with the ambition to *rule the world.*

In the *Los Angeles Times*, T. R. Cassel vented his pessimistic assessment of the American presidential race of 1980. Considering the two front-runners, he called one "disastrously incompetent," and the other, a "bungler of simplistic exaggerations." He was sure that "nobody knows what to do. We have no direction. I know the odds. Next January when the President is spouting the predictable inauguration tripe, I'll be on the first leg of a lonely journey around the world in search of Atlantis."

Whether Cassel is right or wrong is not the issue. It's that so many in the West today feel this way about democratic leaders. People want someone to come down from the sky, or up from beneath, and seize the reins.

That is precisely what is going to happen!

The nearly universal fear is that man can't make it on his own. For several months in the late 1970s, the film *The Antichrist* was widely publicized in Western Europe and North America. This, of course, stimulated people to ask, "What *is* the 'Antichrist'?" Certainly, their imaginings produced a spectrum of possibilities. Would the Antichrist be a Charles Manson, an Ayatollah Khomeini, an Idi Amin, a Madalyn Murray O'Hare or a Jim Jones? Would it be a man, a woman, a god, or a devil? A "peacenik," a warmonger, or only a buffoon?

The movie was filmed on location in Italy where the ancient Roman Empire was headquartered; for centuries, Bible scholars have predicted that this empire will revive and out of it will rise a "beast." This beast, the Antichrist, will rise to power so legitimately and peacefully that the world will never suspect the evil power behind him. Once the reins of power are in his grasp, he will exploit his combination of military genius and hypnotic influence to bring a bewildered world under his heel quickly.

Another recent box office hit was *The Omen*, which depicted the Antichrist in childhood. *Time* observed that the movie was "rendered believable by the total conviction with which it is told." It also noted that the movie "rests on the biblical prophecy about the return of the Prince of Darkness taken from *The Revelation* to fit certain events of our time—the creation of Israel and the Common Market." The magazine concluded that these are "times to believe in a reincarnated Devil."

Although belief in the coming of Antichrist has been most visibly held by evangelicals, it has never been their private domain. It is a prophetic biblical teaching which originated in Judaism, at least from the time of Daniel onward. In *The Dictionary of the Bible* (James Hastings, ed. Scribner, 1963), which enjoys wide mutual acceptance by Protestants, Catholics, and Jews, "Antichrist" is defined as:

> The great opponent and counterpart of the true Messiah, by whom he is finally to be con-

quered. . . . The idea was present in Judaism and developed with the growth of the Messianic hope. . . . While the precise term Antichrist is lacking in Jewish literature, the idea of an opponent who persecutes God's people and is ultimately to be conquered by the Messiah is an integral part of the general hope, born in Prophetism. . . . [The] idea may fairly be said to have been in Daniel 11:26 . . . also Zechariah 12:14.

According to the Talmud, an authority to which Jews frequently refer, the Antichrist was to be named Armilus, a variation of Romulus. He makes war on the messiah, son of Joseph, and slays him, but is in turn destroyed by the messiah, son of David.

The New Catholic Encyclopedia (Publishers Guild, 1966) indicates:

Catholic theologians have been nearly unanimous in maintaining that the Antichrist will be an individual person. . . . The Antichrist is preserved for the "last times," his tyranny to "extend" to the second coming of Jesus Christ. . . .

The Dictionary of the Bible further notes that there has been an expectation of a coming "super-human figure, Satanic in power and character, who was to be head of the opposition both to the people of Christ and to Christ Himself. . . . He was not a general tendency but a definite personality."

Our final authority on this solemn and terribly relevant theme is, of course, the Bible. In 1 John 2:18 we are assured that "antichrist shall come." The Bible is replete with prophecies of the Antichrist. Various names, titles, and descriptions are accorded him in the Scriptures. The Apostle Paul identifies him in 2 Thessalonians 2 as "that man of sin." In the same passage he is called "that wicked one," "the son of perdition," "the man doomed to destruction," "the lawless one."

In Revelation 13, where we find one of the fullest accounts of his wicked activities, he is referred to as "the beast" whose number is 666. In Daniel, where he is described most fully, he is the "little horn" of chapter 7, the "king of fierce countenance" of chapter 8, "the prince that shall come" of chapter 9, and "the willful king" of chapter 11.

Antichrist will be a counterfeit of Jesus Christ. Christ is God; Antichrist will claim to be god. Christ made His way to Jerusalem, died there, descended into hell, and rose again; Antichrist will die, descend into hell, and rise again. Christ inspires worship from His followers; Antichrist will demand—and get—worship. Christ performed signs, miracles, and wonders on behalf of the Kingdom of God; Antichrist will perform ostensible signs, miracles, and wonders on behalf of the kingdom of Satan.

Conversely, there is a distinct contrast between Christ and the Antichrist. Christ came from heaven (John 6:38); the Antichrist will come from hell (Rev. 11:7). Christ came in His Father's name; the Antichrist will come in his own (John 5:43). Christ humbled himself (Phil. 2:8); the Antichrist will exalt himself (2 Thess. 2:4). Christ was despised and afflicted; the Antichrist will be admired and lauded (Rev. 13:3, 4). Christ came to do His Father's will (John 6:38); the Antichrist will come to do his own (Dan. 11:36). Christ came to save (Luke 19:10); the Antichrist will come to destroy (Dan. 8:24). Christ is the Good Shepherd (John 10); the Antichrist will be the evil shepherd (Zech. 11:16, 17). Christ is the Truth (John 14:6); the Antichrist will be "the lie" (2 Thess. 2:11). Christ is "the Mystery of Godliness"—God manifest in the flesh (1 Tim. 3:16); the Antichrist will be "the mystery of iniquity"—Satan manifest in the flesh (2 Thess. 2:7, 9).

A careful reading of Scripture will reveal that the Antichrist shall appear, initially, as a negotiator of peace treaties, offering an anguished and angry world a formula for human harmony. Bishop Fulton Sheen announced before his death that "The Antichrist" will come "talking of peace, prosperity and plenty."

Relevant to this forewarning (which parallels Scripture) are Pope John Paul II's comments on the Soviet invasion of Afghanistan. He noted that the world cannot but have grave "suspicions of the sincerity of declarations in support of peaceful co-existence" when, in actuality, words of "peace, peace" often mean "sudden destruction."

The usually liberal *Toronto Star* carried an editorial which asserted that not "even by Moscow's standards have there been many propaganda exercises to match its present 'peace and brotherhood' offensive." The *Star* goes on to note that "since 1975, when it signed the Helsinki pledge to uphold peace and decent international manners, Moscow has been using guns and armies. . . to gobble up every new territory."

As Pope John Paul II has suggested, today's peace propaganda is more likely a surreptitious announcement that the propagandist is simply buying time for another gross act of aggression.

This whole play of "peace, peace, when there is no peace" is window dressing to which we desperately need to be alert. The Apostle Paul warned the Thessalonians of this very phenomenon: "When they shall say, Peace and safety; then sudden destruction cometh upon them" (1 Thess. 5:3).

When the Pope addressed the United Nations in 1979, he lamented, "Continual preparations for war demonstrated by ever more sophisticated weapons . . . shows the desire for war. . . . Sometime, somewhere, somehow, someone can set in motion the terrible mechanism of general destruction." If the Soviets can make so clever a mockery of the current yearning for peace, what will a satanic wizard, the Antichrist, be able to do? His scheming will eventually arouse the nations of the world to one giant catastrophic battle—Armageddon.

Some think this is an absurd view of biblical prophecy dreamed up by a handful of obscure fundamentalist Protestants. However, it has been a basic Christian belief down through Church history. Though this teaching was much neglected during the Medieval era, it was revived by Spanish Jesuit, Father Franciscus Ribera, in the late sixteenth century. It penetrated Protestantism principally through Anglican theologian Samuel R. Maitland early in the nineteenth century. This teaching is widely accepted throughout the Christian world.

One of the most basic points of this view of prophecy concerns the revival of the Roman Empire, reappearing as a ten-nation European confederacy. The astounding fact is that the European Parliament is now composed of elected representatives of *ten united countries* (Greece, the tenth, was formally admitted in January, 1981). Amazingly, the official publication of the Common Market, *The European Community*, states that "the EC [European Community] Rome treaty supports the interpretation of the books of Ezekiel, Daniel, and Revelation that this 'last days' Kingdom is a new Roman Empire."

When the headquarters for the Common Market were built in Brussels, though only six members existed at the time, ten flagpoles were erected in front of the structure. Ten years ago, EC insiders admitted that there may be further associate members, but that ten senior member nations is the number at which the body wishes to stabilize. Of course, many Bible scholars contend that the Antichrist himself will come up out of an eleventh uniting nation as "the little horn" and that perhaps there are to be thirteen nations involved, with three dropping out or merging with others.

When former Secretary of state Edmund Muskie implored the EC to join the United States in a united front against Iran holding the American hostages, Belgium's Foreign Minister Henri Simonet replied, "As an ally who wishes to be considered faithful, I must say if the leadership is not always understood, it is because there has not always been much to understand." Even the leaders acknowledge a dearth of leadership!

Britain's Roy Jenkins, President of the new EC Parliament, declared to that body that their common yearning was for a "single voice" to represent them all. The world does not simply desire leadership. It desires *one* leader.

The EC is not, as yet, in perfect unity; but as an editorial in the *Los Angeles Times* stated in 1980, the Common Market is probably in better shape to act in concert than it ever has been during its twenty-five-year existence. Uniform governmental policies, coinage, and passports are all nearing reality. If the EC *is* the revived Roman Empire of which the Bible prophesies, it would seem that the stage is nearly ready for the Antichrist to make his appearance.

The Antichrist will make a covenant with the state of Israel for seven years to guarantee their peace (Dan. 9:27; 11:30). Then in the middle of these seven years, he will break the covenant and desecrate the Temple, which will have been restored. After this come the apocalyptic events of the Great Tribulation which are described in Revelation 5-18.

Many Bible commentators believe that about the middle of that tribulation period, a nation "from the north parts"—possibly Russia—will march on Israel (Ezek. 38, 39). The armies of this invader will be utterly destroyed through God's intervention. If this *is* Russia, such destruction would certainly fit the warning that "the nation and kingdom that will not serve thee shall perish" (Isa. 60:12). A theological bleeding heart might protest, claiming that the God of love would never permit this to happen to the Soviets. In fact, it's because He is a God of grace that He would likely so act, since unchecked communism simply continues to propagate and inflict its atheism on increasing millions.

Many overlook the fact that the USSR is the first major world power in history to base their system on atheistic principles. Other empires have been polytheistic but never before totally atheistic. In a news release following a space program success, the Soviets proudly announced, "Our rocket has bypassed the moon. It is nearing the sun and we have not discovered God. We have turned out lights in heaven that no man will be able to put on again. . . . Christ [is] relegated to mythology."

According to a report in the *Los Angeles Times* in 1980, the Soviets have dramatically stepped up efforts to eliminate belief in God from within their boundaries by attempting to brand Christians and Jews as "dissidents" and "undesirable elements." If God's promises are true, judgment will fall on such a nation.

During the time of the Great Tribulation the Antichrist will die—"he shall be destroyed, neither in anger, nor in battle" (Dan. 11:20)—and miraculously, by the infusion of the life of Satan, rise again to life—"And in his estate shall stand up a vile person" (Dan. 11:20).

In collusion with the False Prophet, in full view of the people of the world (TV currently can be transmitted directly from satellites into home receivers), the Antichrist will slay the two witnesses in the streets of Jerusalem. He will be in the final throes of militarily conquering the world when the armies of all the nations gather in the Valley of Megiddo—Armageddon.

Although people laughed at the one-liner by a TV actor—"I don't want to be disturbed by anything short of Armageddon"—this was a backhanded admission that Armageddon seems ominously near. It is at this time that Christ will return to rule on earth, to bring peace and prosperity after unparalleled bloodshed.

Prime Minister Begin of Israel was right when he said that the only ultimate answer to the "pressures of our current situation" is for the "Messiah" to come "and rescue us." He will!

Chapter Three

"That spirit of antichrist" (1 John 4:3)

The Apostle John informed us that prior to Christ's coming again, and even prior to the Antichrist's appearance, there would be "that spirit of antichrist" which "should come" (1 John 4:3).

When I was in England early in 1980, much media attention was being given to the new form of music called Punk Rock. The Pistols were the rock group that gave rise to this movement, and their theme song, "Anarchy in the U.K.," declared: "I am antichrist, I am an anarchist. Don't know what I want, but I know how to get—I wanna destroy."

A journalist commented in *Time* that Punk Rock is a "perversion," noting that anyone who would wear raw meat on the front of his costume is attempting to do more than rebel.

Rock music has generated a strange phenomenon in our society, the extent of which nobody, I expect, knows. Charles Manson claimed he decided to proclaim himself Christ while listening to the Beatles. The *Paris Le Monde*, after Elvis

Presley died, referred to him as the first "Demon of Rock." It seems obvious that rock music has played a significant role in the rise of the "spirit of antichrist."

North Americans—and the people of the whole world—are spiritually restless. On the May 1980 evening that the Quebec Referendum was held, Prime Minister Trudeau of Canada commented to the media that the tragedy of our times was the fact that "the incredible spiritual wealth which is ours in this country" has been dissipated in lost causes.

According to a mid-1979 Gallup poll, 48% of North Americans were deeply cynical and pessimistic about the future. A year later this figure had skyrocketted to an amazing 87%.

The *New York Times* published a survey, in which, on a psychological "Richter scale of hopes and fears (with 1 representing the worst fears and 10 representing the highest hopes), the average American puts himself at 4.8 today, compared with 6.4 five years ago." This was interpreted as "a profound sense of disillusionment, even despondency."

A former Vice President of the United States reflected recently, "One wonders at times whether we are dealing with a world of science, or a world of superstition and fear." An ill-disguised "totalitarian power is gaining ground . . . we have faced no comparable challenges to our way of life—our very existence—in all our history."

News analyst James Reston, in a plea for a leader to appear, bewailed that there is deep "disenchantment of so many people with the secular world. . . . All the other political and economic gods have failed." Therefore the world is ripe for someone to rise "above all the contending races and nations as a solitary figure, with the ability to speak" for us all, "not only as a spiritual but as a political force in the world." The Antichrist will pose as just that—an aspirant to dominate the world spiritually and politically.

Richard Sennett is a social psychologist at New York University. He reckons in his book, *Authority*, that moderns, taking their lead from the French and American revolutions, have attempted over two centuries to emancipate themselves. However, this has left them not in a state of "liberty" but in a state of "alienation" and "impoverishment" of spirit. A prevalent "narcissism" could well "create a Hitler" with precursory "tyrants" showing the way. He is, with uncanny accuracy, describing the scenario which gives rise to the appearance of the Antichrist.

Prince Philip, addressing the Duke of Edinburgh Commonwealth Study Conference with delegates from 32 countries, declared that "mankind can solve technical problems but has failed to cope" with his "racial, linguistic and religious" problems. He also maintained that "only individuals can feel content" through intact "relationship" with God and other people. But otherwise, our universal problems are currently way over our heads.

An indication that many people are unable to cope with the world's problems is the spiraling increase in the suicide rate. A bestseller in England is Nicholas Reed's *Exit*, a manual on how to commit suicide. The book has evoked phenomenal response from readers. According to an AP account, "Flooding into a basement office in London's Kensington district are thousands of letters from people who want to know how to kill themselves."

Expressing his own hopelessness, British pop star Adam Faith said that if in the 1980s "someone gave me a ticket on a plane to Mars, I'd take it, and worry about the consequences afterwards."

What about people who don't consider suicide a valid option? Where are they going for solutions? They are not only looking around for a leader, but they are looking upward to the stars; whatever we've thought in our loftier intellectual moments about the rule of rational minds over man's affairs, the fact is, Western man is turning to the occult. According to a Gallup poll, 77% of the people in our society have gone to the trouble to learn what astrological sign they were born under, 24% read astrological columns daily and 22% "believe" in the credibility of astrological forecasts.

Under the headline, "Growing Antichrist Movement in This Country," the *Minneapolis Tribune* published the viewpoint that since Christianity has been effectively abolished from the schools, it is inevitably necessary "to infiltrate our schools with the occult." This would seem to be but one step away from society's bending the knee before the shrine of Antichrist.

But would sophisticated Westerners actually "worship the image of the beast," as the Bible indicates? The evidence points strongly to that possibility. "I just adore him! I just worship him!" a teenage girl screamed when she saw her favorite singer from the Bay City Rollers in Toronto. In a Canadian appearance by the rock group Teen-Age Head, a thousand unticketed youths pelted police with beer bottles and fire crackers, jumped gates and swam the moat at Ontario Place to try and reach their idols.

A few years ago when the Beatles dominated the rock music scene, their press agent, Derek Taylor, commented on the public reaction they evoked: "It's absolutely rude, profane, vulgar. . . . They are completely antichrist." He described a typical scene: "Sick people rushed up. It was as if some savior had arrived. The only thing left for the Beatles to do is to go on a healing tour. I'm antichrist, but these boys even shock me."

The general public is spiritually gullible. If the Antichrist appears offering answers to the world's problems, people will, enmasse, follow him. The Bible says that nearly all will wonder, then, wander after the Beast—like so many lemmings heading for the sea.

Not long before his death, the late Walter Lippmann lamented that, "for us all the world is disorderly and dangerous, ungoverned and apparently ungovernable." Into such a vacuum, the Antichrist will step and seize the reins of power.

As these disturbing conditions are on the rise, democracy is on the wane. Richard Gwyn writes, "Pessimism is fashionable these days; democracy, it is said, no longer works and the public's mood is that of a 'lynch mob.'"

Alexandr Solzhenitsyn warns those of us in the West, "You have the impression that democracies can last . . . but democracies are islands lost in an immense river of history. The water is always rising. You have forgotten the meaning of liberty. When you acquired liberty, it was a sacred notion [but] you have forgotten," he chides. "Liberty without obligation and responsibility" cannot survive, because today throughout the Free World, "nobody is ready to die for it." Solzhenitsyn gives the world five years at most before there is a nuclear war.

Few today who observe the world seriously could doubt that Solzhenitsyn is right. Vigilance is down and apathy is up. Ours seems to be an age of selfishness and carelessness. Professor Samuel Huntington of Harvard calls this abandonment of concern the "democratic distemper" of the day.

Freedom House is an American group of intellectuals, which for a quarter-century has been watchdogging the world in the interests of human liberty, assessing the ebb and flow of current civil and political freedoms. The organization reckons that whereas in 1974, 58% of the world's population lived under political systems considered democratic, today this number has been reduced to a frightening 19%. Henry Kissinger judges that there are only twenty surviving democracies in the world.

Many Canadians were alarmed when their Prime Minister asserted that the future of their country requires "a massive intervention into the decision-making power" through the whole height and depth of our free enterprise system. Such a massive intervention could well beckon dictatorship.

After his return to power in 1980, Prime Minister Trudeau holidayed in Jamaica. While there, it was reported that he and longtime intimate Michael Manley concurred on "the need for a new world economic order." They were right. The Antichrist will offer such an order. But his program will turn what order is left into chaos.

So what is the answer? Our wonderful hope is that Jesus Christ will finally come and establish His new order.

During the 1980s, much attention will be focused on the Third World—whether democracy or dictatorship will emerge triumphant. All signs point toward the latter. I am particularly sad to see nations such as Angola become Communist, in light of the fact that my fellow-Canadians have sent large numbers of missionaries (highest per capita in the world over the last 50 years) to Africa to evangelize and educate the people.

Missionary efforts in such places will no longer exist if Communist dictators have their way. Tyndale House Publishers report that the new regime in Angola is already curtailing the distribution of Bibles in that country. Much of Africa is currently in the throes of complex political turmoil. As inevitable change takes place, it is hoped that the baby will not be thrown out with the bath water; that as one set of shackles is shed, another set, far more oppressive and cruel, will not be imposed.

In the Far East, South Korea and the Philippines have swung sharply to the right; North Korea, Vietnam, and Cambodia to the left; India, Indonesia and Thailand are looking both ways. Observers of Mainland China see an unpredictable, swinging pendulum. People are craving authority and order.

In a recent issue of *U.S. News and World Report*, eight leading intellectuals explained that people in chaos, when faced with a choice between order or freedom, will always choose order. This is one of the main reasons that, since

World War II, more than half of the world's governments have been overthrown by coups d'etat.

And our situation is chaotic. UN Secretary-General Kurt Waldheim declared, "I do not wish to seem overdramatic, but I can only conclude from the information that is available to me as Secretary-General that the members of the United Nations have perhaps ten years left in which to subordinate their ancient quarrels and launch a global partnership to curb the arms race, to improve the human environment, to defuse the population explosion, and to supply the required momentum to world development efforts." The alternative is a situation "beyond our capacity to control."

We can be quite certain, though, that the United Nations will not become the kingdom base for the Antichrist to take over, by the nature of Waldheim's statement. When asked how the UN could police its will and turn its pronouncements into law, Waldheim replied wryly, "Like the Pope, I have no divisions."

Bertrand Russell said that we must very soon have world government or universal annihilation. The late Arnold Toynbee reckoned that man in his present panic is "ripe for the deifying of any new Caesar who might succeed in giving the world unity and peace."

Dr. Henry Spaak, statesman from Belgium, expressed, "The truth is that the method of international committees has failed," and consequently "the highest order of experience" indicates that only a world ruler can control the world. "Let him come, and let him come quickly," and "galvanize all governments" and "let him vanquish" anarchy from the earth. Spaak is recognized as a prime advocate of the reunification of Europe.

An open letter to the Carter administration from a representative European recently appeared in *Time*. The writer appealed, "In virtually every capital you will hear a litany of the European Community's grim complaints. England is at a standstill. France seems to be in disarray. . . . Italy has a crisis government. Germany can't rally a world cause." In Western Europe, there are "no leaders of government claiming they want more room for unilateral action. . . . The acerbic rhetoric of 1973-74 seems to be gone for good. Unfortunately, it has been replaced by an atmosphere of almost total policy paralysis. . . . One ranking officer in the Council of Europe describes his organization as a 'walking cadaver.' Another says that 'the governments "of the ten" are now expending all of their energies simply to stay in power.' " Such a vacuum is ideal for the rise of a world leader.

The possibility for the entrance of such a leader is acknowledged to be imminent. Prince Philip cautioned the British Institute of Directors that unless emergency measures are taken to pull Britain together, the whole building of state will collapse. Then Britain would become a

"Communist-bloc type country."

During Britain's most recent election, Conservative M. P. Enoch Powell warned his fellow Britons, "This is the . . . last election at which the British people will be given an opportunity to decide whether their country is to remain a democratic nation, governed by the will of its own electorate expressed in its own Parliament, or whether it will become one province in a new European super-state under institutions which know nothing of the political rights and liberties that we have so long taken for granted." Powell is probably not fully aware of the prophetic quality of his words.

The governments of Western Europe have become increasingly unstable. *Time* has noted that during the last few years, every nation in the Common Market has undergone a change of leadership. The magazine observes, "Being a leader in any country is no great fun these days. All industrial societies face intractable problems that the leadership is not capable of coping with." Here lies the appeal for, say, Western Europe to unite under one man, if he has the charisma to inspire wide-spread confidence. *Time* admits, "The real aim of the Market [EC] is, of course, to become one single country."

Obviously, the "spirit of Antichrist" is already prevalent, in the mood of the people, and in the political climate. The Antichrist would not, in such a state of affairs, face a very difficult task in getting on first base—Europe.

Chapter Four

"Now are there many antichrists; whereby we know that it is the last time" (1 John 2:18).

R. S. Parson wrote in *Time* that if "the end of the world is at hand," if we are surely approaching "The Second Coming," if

> . . . these are the last days, we need to be looking for Jesus' sure prophecy. . . , "Then if anyone says to you, 'There He is!' do not believe it. For false Christs and false prophets will arise and show great signs and wonders, so as to lead astray, if possible, even the elect."

Parson is, of course, quoting Matthew 24:23-26. When Jesus was asked by His disciples for a sign that He would soon be back, He replied that the very first thing to watch for were Christ-quacks, God-pretenders, and Messiah-masqueraders. "Take heed that no man deceive you. For many shall come in my name, saying, I am Christ; and shall deceive many" (Matt. 24:4, 5).

It seems, from Scripture, that the many false Christs will be narrowed down until there is one of superstar stature—the Antichrist. In the book of Daniel we are given a surprisingly complete description of his origin, rise to power, the highlights of his wicked domination, and his ultimate destruction.

Meanwhile, we are told to watch for "many antichrists" who will come "in the last time," according to 1 John 2:18. If this were the only sign we were to watch for, in anticipation of Christ's return, the current events would point strongly to its imminence. Syracuse University Professor Agehananda Bharati, after researching the contemporary situation, announced that there are fully 2,000 practicing gurus posing as Christs. Billy Graham recently stated that currently there are at least 400 Christ-imposters in Los Angeles alone.

Harvard's Professor Harvey Cox believes that this is the "age of the instant gurus, when any nabob with a half complacent public relations staff is assured of a covey of Western devotees the moment he announces his divinity." The trend is so rampant that, according to a recent report, nearly 25 million North Americans have been swept into these Christ-pretending cults in the last decade. If one out of nine in our society has been duped into following one of these charlatans, we need to look for a moment at some of the most influential ones.

Certainly the most publicized of the recent Christ-pretenders was the horrifying and tragic figure Jim Jones. As he exploited the ministry the church had granted him, he gathered around him a thousand devotees, 913 of whom followed him in a mass suicide in Guyana during November, 1978. Even at the time of his ordination, Jones threw down his Bible on the platform and screamed to his devotees that they were to listen to *him*, not to the Word of God. He was proclaiming himself as their christ.

Very prominent in the "christ business" have been the gurus from the East. Until the group was recently banned from Chicago's O'Hare Airport, on any given day one could be accosted by fifty Hare Krishna devotees, in comparison to one Christian witness who might make an approach. When A. C. Bhaktivedanti Swami Prabhupāda, leader of the Western Krishna movement, came to Toronto, a reporter wrote:

> Followers threw themselves to the floor to kiss the feet of the small, flower-wreathed, dhoti-clad figure. . . . The founder of the International Society for Krishna Consciousness was greeted by the clashing of cymbals, the beating of hand drums, the bugle-like shriek of conch shells, and the waving of peacock and yak-tail fans.

Though sophisticated people smugly smile, the Hare Krishna followers take themselves very seriously. When they make appearances on TV, their spokesmen are polished and persuasive.

No less aggressive are the people of the Divine Light Mission, whose Guru Maharaj Ji openly proclaims himself the "Christ incarnate." According to the organization's press releases, his followers number ten million.

Having a profound effect on North American society is the Transcendental Meditation (TM) movement, led by the Maharishi Mahesh Yogi. This cult has been featured on the cover of *Time*; and, under the pretense of not being a religion, it has received funding from the U.S. government. Anyone who enters the world of TM, however, soon discovers that the Maharashi privately claims to be an "incarnate christ," who came from, and is returning to, God. Ten years ago, former Beatle George Harrison, riding the current of the "Jesus Movement," made a lucrative hit with his hymn to the Maharishi, singing, "My sweet lord, really want to know you; really want to show you, love." A prominent ingredient in the song is a "hallelujiah-Hare Krishna" descant, surely connoting worship.

Time has pointed to "incontrovertible evidence that TM is merely a subtly disguised form of Hinduism," that the "mantra," given by the TM instructor as a chant, is invariably the name of a Hindu god.

The Maharishi even made the preposterous claim that totally committed TM'ers could, when in deep meditation, levitate as high as fourteen feet off the ground and remain suspended for indefinite periods of time.

Another "christ" has appeared in recent years from Korea—Sun Myung Moon—who allegedly has 20 million followers convinced that he is the Messiah. His Unification Church is one of the amazing religious phenomena of our time; New York City is a long way from Seoul, but Moon can reportedly draw a crowd of 50,000 to hear his message.

In a recent edition of the *London Telegraph*, an article revealed how a brilliant Ph.D. candidate, Paul Stuart-Kregor, just short of his degree, dropped out to become a fanatical "Moonie," out to convert everyone in sight. Such aggressiveness results from Moon's ambition to take over the world as "the messiah." He constantly reminds his followers, "I am your mind."

When I was in Jamaica for crusades in 1980, I discovered that the Rastafarian sect is a real menace. Even in Toronto, 3,000 of the 160,000 Jamaicans there are followers of a "black messiah, their own special christ," who will eventually appear to lead them out of bondage into the promised land of black dominance in the world.

One of America's own gurus is Charles Manson, whose fiendish antics have held news readers spellbound for over a decade, even though the man has very few acknowledged disciples. Lynne (Squeaky) Fromme, who allegedly attempted to assassinate former President Gerald Ford, announced to the world on behalf of the Mansonites, "We're nuns now, and we wear red robes. We're waiting for our Lord, and there's only one thing to do before he comes off the cross, and that's clean up the earth. Our red robes are an example of the blood of the sacrifice." Manson's disciples want Charlie out of jail so that as their christ he can become king of the world.

David Miller, in his book *The New Polytheism: Rebirth of the Gods and Goddesses*, correctly assesses the social climate when he writes that college students currently demand "massive and total access to all the gods of men, Eastern and Western, primitive and modern, heretical and orthodox, mad and sane."

Sharing the limelight with these obviously unorthodox groups are the business-like and subtly destructive new-consciousness and self-awareness seminars. One of the most outrageous of these is est (Erhard Seminars Training), originated by Werner Erhard, guru deluxe. His high-voltage presentations, which are a mixture of Zen, Scientology, Transcendental Meditation, and a smattering of other Eastern cults, are a sly affront to the Judeo-Christian view of reality.

Students at the seminars are promised that they will "get it"—whatever "it" is. They are continually subjected to verbal abuse, and told they "are all [obscenity]." "Don't analyze or judge, just realize!" the trainer yells. Two weekends (for a total of 60 hours) and $350 later, the "graduates" are turned loose on the world, convinced that life is a game and that "whatever is, is."

Until nine years ago, Werner Erhard was a

bumbling seeker named John Paul Rosenberg, who deserted his wife and four children in Philadelphia and went west to make it big. He did. Today est is a $25-million-a-year sensation, with 300,000 graduates, many of whom are prominent social figures.

Then there is the reflective, charming Michael Murphy, who extols the benefits of H.P.M. (which has nothing to do with horsepower ratings). H.P.M. stands for Human Potential Movement. Murphy leads his disciples into the "great opening up, a synthesis between the intuition and the intellect, body and mind, matter and spirit, East and West." He promises the students brand new lives if they will undergo transformation from competition to acquiesence, from aggression to gentleness, from acquisition to sharing, from dominance to blending, and from materialism to humanism.

Murphy's pitch is especially appealing to the Utopian-minded. But, it is like trying to live the beatitudes without Christ. Michael Murphy plus H.P.M. does not spell the millennium.

Another of these Madison Avenue-style cults is the International Transactional Analysis Association. The group jets its 600 delegates into the Hilton Inn in San Francisco to purr their "I'm OK, You're OK" clichés at each other for several days. Their advertised discussions center around such themes as "The Theory of the Goopy Three-Layer Cake," "Rackets and

Games," "Self-stroking," and, for the more seri-ous-minded, "As the Onion Is Peeled, So Shall You Grow."

The success of all these cults indicates that Western man is searching for a god, and he eas-ily believes whoever talks fast enough or con-vincingly enough to outwit him. Sociologist Rod-ney Stark, who published a survey on the cults, observes that the cults "are much more magical than the established . . . Christian churches ever were." Especially young people fall prey to the Pied Pipers that feign "science" to gain "re-spectability," and these include "astrology, transcendental meditation, psychic practition-ers, occultism . . . scientology and the Moon-ies."

Most people wish they had within them and wish that we as a society could contrive the con-ditions for universal harmony. But, much to their frustration, they are discovering that Uto-pia is a place to which no one can get without a messiah. Therefore, people not only follow after self-proclaimed gods, but sophisticated Western man continually creates his own god-heroes. In the past we had Flash Gordon, Superman, Tar-zan, Captain Marvel and the Green Hornet. Contemporary successors include "The Invisible Man," "The Marathon Man," and "The Man Who Fell to Earth."

Due to the success of the "Six Million Dollar Man," we have been granted a "trinity" of bionic saviors—the Bionic Man, the Bionic Woman, and the Bionic Boy. Lee Majors as the Bionic Man is portrayed as an astronaut who, when returning from space, lost his legs, and arm and an eye. Bionic limbs and a special "eye" empower him to detect needs at incredible distances, to operate like a machine, to go through walls like a cannonball—all for the purpose of rescuing the victimized.

The Bionic Woman loses her limbs in a parachuting accident, actually dies and revives, then takes on her new superhuman role as emacipator and redeemer.

The Bionic Boy, Andy, loses his mortal legs in a rockslide and assumes bionic ones that can kick a football 100 yards and scale a thousand-foot cliff.

The ultimate of these media-produced demigods, of course, is Superman, who swoops in from outer space in the costliest film ever produced by Hollywood. He circles the earth in ninety seconds, rescues a cat in peril, and saves the President in his Air Force One from certain death. He thwarts an earthquake catastrophe and delivers civilization from an impending nuclear disaster.

What are all these but modern Greeks attempting to deify a Hercules? Dr. Charles Beck of the University of Calgary observed that this "craze for the Bionic Woman, Kojak, Police Woman, King Kong, astrology, and the macho-gun subculture" is simply man scanning the skies for a messiah. Canadian geneticist Dr. David Suzuki concurs with that very conclusion, and he has long been asking when that "authoritarian personality" will appear.

The Canadian concludes that everyone these days is either seeking to worship a hero or seeking to be a hero. People will do nearly anything to grab at greatness. In the Acts of the Apostles we read of Samaria's messiah-figure, Simon, a mini-antichrist, who "used sorcery, and bewitched the people of Samaria, giving out that himself was some great one: to whom they all gave heed, from the least to the greatest, saying, This man is the great power of God" (Acts 8:9, 10). The only difference between today and the first century is that, thanks to the mass media, adulation of a personality is no longer a community phenomenon but a worldwide rage.

In Canada the latest superhero is the "Great Gretsky," the most charisma-imbued, athletically endowed hockey star since Bobby Orr. According to a reporter, when Gretsky visited a zoo in 1980, a multitude of fans coerced him to hold "court amid the mandrils and palm trees of the African pavillion—and worshippers waited up to an hour to see him."

The admiration accorded to this athlete is so absurdly religious that Rex McLeod wrote in the *Toronto Star*, ". . . the star shining in the east heralded the arrival of Gretsky."

There is hardly a more egotistical vaunting of self than that of Muhammad Ali, who proclaims himself as "the greatest." In the film about him, *The Greatest,* none other than Ali, "the greatest," plays the leading role. Jim Murray, sports columnist, quipped, "He'll hardly be satisfied 'til Michelangelo paints him on the Vatican ceiling."

But even "the greatest" can sometimes be out-gunned. It is alleged that when Ali recently was aboard a plane waiting for take-off, the attendant asked him to buckle his seatbelt. He replied, "I'm superman. I don't need no seatbelt!" The woman retorted, triumphantly, "If you were superman, Mr. Ali, you wouldn't need no plane!"

Arnold Schwarzenegger, the Austrian who currently holds the Mr. Universe title, was once "a 95-pound weakling." Then he religiously devoted himself to body-building because, "I just wanted to be the greatest in something. In grammar school, I was dreaming about being some dictator of a country or some savior like Jesus."

When 50,000 to 60,000 teenagers gave screaming adulation to the Bay City Rollers recently in Toronto, the memory of Beatlemania suddenly seemed like soggy toast in comparison. The *Toronto Star* noted, "Adolph Hitler would have given his last pair of jackboots to be able to manipulate children with the skill of the Rollers."

"You're a god—a demi-god at least!" the guest cooed to his smug-faced host, Johnny Carson, on the *Tonight* show. He was pleading with the superstar to stop smoking because he is so widely emulated by millions of nightly viewers. It is pathetic to see how feebly such superstars resist this flattery.

A *Newsweek* cover story cited John Denver as "the most popular pop singer in America." Denver flatly stated, "One of these days I'll be so complete I won't be a human. I'll be a god."

As I observe the people of our society, many of them highly sophisticated, I find it curious, as well as tragic, that they are so easily seduced by the world's aspiring gods and goddesses. To me, it is a demonstration of how near they are to falling on their knees before an antichrist.

As people reject the real, but invisible God and bow to mortal or media-devised gods, the ideas they accept as truth become more and more satanic. They believe the occult-related concepts from movies such as *The Omen* or *Rosemary's Baby,* but view the doctrines of Scripture as nonsense. Film critic Clyde Gilmour wrote concerning *The Omen*: "You don't have to be either religious or superstitious to find your scalp tingling again and again during its 109 minutes. *The Omen* could scare the [expletive deleted] out of an atheist."

In *Rosemary's Baby,* a child is conceived by Satan, which people, amidst the rise of the occult, find increasingly acceptable. Yet, the virgin birth is scoffed at. I find this an omen of the future, or, as the title of H. G. Wells' book states, "The Shape of Things to Come."

Chapter Five

"This is a deceiver and an antichrist" (2 John 7).

Franklin A. McKnight wrote in 1980—and it could have been written in an editorial anywhere—"I . . . now have little doubt that the climate in this country is being prepared not so much for a bloodbath as for a brute of a dictator."

Antichrist's tracks are today imprinting man's trail ahead; the yet unidentified beast seems to be treading through the murky night of human society. People are terrified, gulping sleeping pills in vain to tranquilize themselves from the present trauma.

I remember on our Saskatchewan farm as a child what excitement I had in finding the tracks of a wolf, a weasel, a badger, or a moose in the fresh snow! It was a spine-chilling challenge to trace those tracks to the animal itself. "The Beast"—the Antichrist—has his own indentations deeply tracked in society today. The jackboots of a jockeying dictator are kicking on the door of humanity, about to break in on the world scene.

Animals have long been used as symbols of nations. In Daniel 7 we read of a lion, a bear, and a leopard symbolizing ancient empires. Today we have the Russian bear, the English bulldog, the American eagle, etc. Modern man, therefore, should have no trouble with references to the Antichrist speaking of "The Beast." It is significant that the two chief "biographers" of the Antichrist—Daniel, whom Jesus referred to as an authority on the subject; and John, who was with Jesus on that occasion—referred most often to him as "the beast."

I can't think of a more frightening encounter any person could have than to meet in gloomy darkness—alone—a snarling, flesh-tearing, fiery-eyed beast. Terrifying, partly because it's so tantalizing, this sort of rendezvous has something of the irresistible fascination for man that a flame has for a moth.

The Antichrist will be "The Beast." Glance at the media and you will see that the masses are infatuated with beasts. The movie houses pack them in with titles like, *The Black Stallion*, *A Man Called Horse*, *Jaws*, *King Kong*, *Tentacles*, *The Eagle Has Landed*, and *The White Buffalo*.

For years on our TV screens we've watched the affluent and arrogant Morris the cat. Then there are the dog heroes—Lassie or Won Ton Ton (who always seems to fly first class). Lady Beaverbrook went one better, chartering a 272-seat jetliner from London to Halifax at a cost of $17,000, just to get her two little dogs over the Atlantic. And on a network TV program, the wanting-to-believe millions watched a woman demonstrate that she and her dog actually talk to each other.

Dr. M. Librach complained in The *Toronto Star*, "When my wife takes our pet dog to the vet, she must pay about twice the amount I receive for an office call. It is interesting that we in Ontario value dogs twice as much as people."

We have long used animal names for our automobiles—cougar, mustang, rabbit, hawk, impala, barracuda, wildcat. And how about professional athletic teams? We have Bruins, Tigers, Rams, Wildcats, and Eagles, to name a few, all with the intention of devouring the competition like hungry animals. After all, who would call his team the Puppies or the Chickens if he wanted to fill up a stadium?

Even in politics, "beastliness" seems to reign; Americans rally to the signs of the elephant and the donkey, and a writer attributed Prime Minister Trudeau's recent victory to his "animal magnetism."

Rupert Murdoch, Australian publishing magnate, expanded his empire to the U.S. by procuring the *New York Post, The Village Voice, New York* magazine, and *The New West* magazine during the 1970s. On the cover of *Time* Murdoch was pictured with his head on the body of a Koala bear. The cover story began with this italicized paragraph:

The National Guard had sealed off lower Manhattan when the great beast was first sighted, and helicopter gunships buzzed like giant killer bees over the East River. But the beast was undeterred. Lusting for some name-less trophy, he climbed down from the top of the *New York Post* building and lumbered up Second Avenue toward the deserted offices of *New York* magazine.

When Johnny Carson announced his new three-year contract with NBC for the *Tonight* show, the UPI circulated a photograph of him dressed as a rabbit. And when you approached the newsstands in 1980, you could hardly miss seeing Walter Sheldon's *The Beast*.

With such "beast-consciousness" around us, it seems quite believable to open to the thirteenth chapter of the Revelation and read of two terrible persons, both called "beasts." One is a ruler on the throne of a universal empire, and the other is the head of a worldwide religious system.

There is an amazing parallel between the Trinity of the Godhead and the trinity of evil presented in Revelation 13. In this chapter Satan appears as opposed to God the Father, the Antichrist flaunts himself against God the Son, and the false prophet is in violent opposition to God the Holy Spirit. The two "beasts" are both, of course, anti-Christian. "And I stood upon the sand of the sea, and saw a beast rise up out of the sea" (Rev. 13:1).

In the Bible the beast is a familiar simile representing a political power. From comparison with the visions of Daniel, we know we are looking here at a revived Roman Empire. It rises "up out of the sea" of the Gentile nations (compare Rev. 17:15 where the symbol of the sea is employed and interpreted), "having seven heads and ten horns."

Seven is the number of completeness; here it probably speaks of universal power and dominion (v. 7). The ten horns correspond with the ten toes of Nebuchadnezzar's dream image, and the ten horns of the fourth beast in Daniel's vision are described in Daniel seven. The ten horns and the ten toes illustrate the ten sub-divisions of the Roman Empire, which will be revived, possibly through the Common Market.

While Europe has been united for over two decades as an economic community (the EC), and is fast evolving into a political confederation, its beginnings can be found in the post-World War II alliance, NATO. Jean Monet, a major force in the establishment of NATO, assured the world (even in the 1950s) that the emerging military alliance would only be totally effective when it had evolved into a political union.

The coming Antichrist will see to it that such a vision is consummated. "And upon his horns ten crowns, and upon his heads the name of blasphemy" (Rev. 13:1). So ten heads of states in Europe will eventually join together in a confederation of nations, under the sovereignty of the Antichrist, and thus constitute the empire, as revealed in Daniel 7:24 and Revelation 17:12.

The beast out of the sea—"which . . . was like unto a leopard, and his feet were as the feet of a bear, and his mouth as the mouth of a lion" (Rev. 13:1, 2)—is the same as the "dreadful and terrible" fourth beast in Daniel 7:7, 8. It is the Roman Empire. The leopard (Dan. 7:6), as well as the rough goat of Daniel 8:5, is the Grecian Empire. The bear of Daniel 7:4 is the Medo-Persian Empire. However, the beast of Revelation 13 is like a leopard, with feet like a bear's, and a mouth like a lion's. This seems to imply that the last great Gentile empire will reflect the spirit of all the Gentile empires which preceded it, including Greece, Medo-Persia and Babylon. A beast is an appropriate symbol of them all.

"And the dragon gave him his power, and his seat, and great authority" (Rev. 13:2). The dragon is Satan himself (Rev. 20:2), and he endues the Antichrist with his own power. The word for "seat" is "thronos," literally "throne"; Satan is, of course, the Prince of this world, according to Jesus (John 12:31; 14:30). The Apostle Paul refers to him as "the prince of the power of the air, the spirit that now worketh in the children of disobedience" (Eph. 2:2). He once offered the kingdoms of the world to the Son of God, who refused his offer (Luke 4:5-8). But in the beast, Satan finds a man—the superman the world clam-

ors for—and to him he gives his throne, power,
and authority:

> And I saw one of his heads as it were
> wounded to death; and his deadly wound was
> healed: and all the world wondered after the
> beast. And they worshipped the dragon which
> gave power unto the beast: and they wor-
> shipped the beast, saying, Who is like unto the
> beast? who is able to make war with him?
> (Rev. 13:3-5)

It is not difficult, as we discussed earlier, to
understand that such a "possessed ruler" would
have the world at his feet. If he were powerful
enough to subdue the nations and quell any re-
sistance, and also exhibit superhuman capabili-
ties, the world would pursue him en masse. And
if the world discovered that his power was actually granted by Satan, people would eagerly worship "the dragon which gave power unto the
beast."

Once God is rejected by society, worship of
Satan will follow closely behind. We shall see in
this chapter how the worship of Antichrist will
become the state religion of the whole earth:
"And there was given unto him a mouth speaking great things and blasphemies; and power
was given unto him to continue forty and two
months" (Rev. 13:5).

The time factor revealed in verse 5 helps us
to locate the manifestation and reign of the Antichrist. The forty-two months are identical in

length to the 1,260 days of the two witnesses from heaven (Rev. 11:3), and to the "time, times, and an half" of Daniel 12:7. The exact parallel is found in Daniel 7:25, where the same "beast" is spoken of; he will "think to change times and laws: and they shall be given into his hand until a time and times and the dividing of time." In Daniel a "time" is a year (the Jewish year had 360 days). These three and one-half years are probably the final years of "the times of the Gentiles" spoken of by Jesus in Luke 21:24. This also may be the time of the Great Tribulation, the latter half of the final seven years.

"And he opened his mouth in blasphemy against God, to blaspheme his name, and his tabernacle, and them that dwell in heaven" (Rev. 13:6). The Antichrist, the mad "man of sin . . . the son of perdition; . . . opposeth and exalteth himself above all that is called God, or that is worshipped; so that he as God sitteth in the temple of God, shewing himself that he is God" (2 Thess. 2:3, 4). His "coming is after the working of Satan with all power and signs and lying wonders, and with all deceivableness of unrighteousness in them that perish" (2 Thess. 2:9, 10). The raptured Church, as well as God himself, will be the objects of his blasphemies. He will blaspheme "them that dwell in heaven." We, who have by faith received Jesus Christ, will be included in that happy company, and Satan's railings will not be able to affect us.

But on the earth, "it was given unto him to make war with the saints, and to overcome them: and power was given him over all kindreds, and tongues, and nations" (Rev. 13:7). The "saints" here are the Jewish remnant of the endtime, together with an innumerable company, out of all the nations (Rev. 7), who have refused to worship the Antichrist and shall die for the testimony of Jesus: "And all that dwell upon the earth shall worship him, whose names are not written in the book of life of the Lamb slain from the foundation of the world" (Rev. 13:8). That will be a time of testing and sifting. It will avail nothing in that day merely to profess to know God. The "form of godliness" will not do.

"If any man have an ear, let him hear. He that leadeth into captivity shall go into captivity: he that killeth with the sword must be killed with the sword. Here is the patience and the faith of the saints" (Rev. 13:9, 10). In these verses God warns His people not to resort to force to establish their rights. Let them wait only on God, who will "avenge them speedily" (Luke 18:8).

"And I beheld another beast coming up out of the earth; and he had two horns like a lamb, and he spake as a dragon" (Rev. 13:11). This beast is the false prophet. It is characteristic of all false prophets to parade themselves as representatives of the Lamb, but teach and preach doctrines of Satan.

"And he exerciseth all the power of the first beast before him, and causeth the earth and them which dwell therein to worship the first beast, whose deadly wound was healed" (Rev. 13:12). This refers back to verse three, where we see one of the beast's heads healed after a mortal wound. As mentioned before, the beast will experience a spectacular death and resurrection, being restored to life by the power of Satan (also see Dan. 11:20). This could also speak of the restoration of the Roman Empire which has been reckoned dead for centuries, but seems destined for resurrection in the EC.

"And he doeth great wonders, so that he maketh fire come down from heaven on the earth in the sight of men" (Rev. 13:13). Though such miracles are mentioned in the Bible, modern man would be prone to relegate such an idea to the myth category. Whether such a phenomenon will be from a technical or supernatural source, we do not know, but it is now possible! Recently the *New York Times* reported that the Russians have developed a laser beam device that can be mounted on an orbiting satellite, and that at any given moment, they could trigger the release of a laser beam flame which would descend in an apocalyptic flash on a predetermined target.

Paul told the Corinthians that "the Jews require a sign," and here is a sign for those who turn from God in that day of trial. It duplicates Elijah's chosen sign on Mount Carmel. It will deceive all but the very elect:

> And deceiveth them that dwell on the earth by the means of those miracles which he had power to do in the sight of the beast; saying to them that dwell on the earth that they should make an image to the beast, which had the wound by a sword and did live. (Rev. 13:14)

This is the third chapter of Daniel all over again. Nebuchadnezzar was the first ruler in the period called the Times of the Gentiles; the Antichrist of the end-time will be the last ruler in that period. Both Nebuchadnezzar and the Antichrist introduce idolatry as the state religion of the world, demanding people worship them under threat of death.

"And he had power to give life unto the image of the beast, that the image of the beast should both speak, and cause that as many as would not worship the image of the beast should be killed" (Rev. 13:15). The word "life" used here should be "breath." This image is no doubt the "abomination of desolation" spoken of by Daniel and by the Lord Jesus. It will be placed in the Holy of Holies of the Tribulation temple at Jerusalem, displacing the ark of the covenant and the mercy seat.

"And he causeth all, both small and great, rich and poor, free and bond, to receive a mark in their right hand or in their foreheads: and that no man might buy or sell, save he that had the mark, or the name of the beast, or the number of his name" (Rev. 13:16,17). The mark of the beast will be the alternative in that day for those who refuse the seal of God on their foreheads (Rev. 7:3). This will be a universal boycott against the faithful followers of Christ. People will either worship the beast or starve. This is not a new concept. The Roman Caesars often proclaimed themselves divine, and demanded to be treated as such. To deny the Caesar's divinity was to invite death. Things will be much the same in the last days.

"Here is wisdom. Let him that hath understanding count the number of the beast: for it is the number of a man; and his number is Six hundred threescore and six" (Rev. 13:18). Here, as well as in Daniel 8 and 11, we have pictures of this dreadful and terrible Antichrist. And parallel to this verse in Revelation, we read in Daniel 12:10, "the wise shall understand."

"The number of man," mentioned in Rev. 13:18, according to scholars, is six. Under the law, man's labor was limited to six days, for God has created man to rest on the seventh day. The seventh is God's day, and seven is the number of divine completeness throughout the Scriptures. The Antichrist's number is a trinity of sixes—666.

Through the Antichrist, Satan seeks to reproduce the works of God; he fails, of course. The Antichrist, after all, is "a man, and not God," though he may "set [his] heart as the heart of God" (Ezek. 28:2).

The number of man was stamped upon the image of Nebuchadnezzar in Daniel 3: it was sixty cubits high and six cubits wide, and its glory was heralded by an orchestra made up of six different instruments. In the image-worship of the end-time, man's number is fully developed, and the result is six and six and six—666.

The destiny of the beast and the false prophet is already clearly determined, according to Rev. 19:20 and 20:10. When Christ returns to judge, He will have them cast alive into the lake of fire. At the end of the Millennium, Satan is cast in to join them as they are "tormented day and night for ever and ever."

Chapter Six

"Then shall that Wicked be revealed"
(2 Thess. 2:8)

The *New Catholic Encyclopedia* observes correctly that all through church history, zealous prophets have presumptuously identified certain characters or movements as "the Antichrist," only to suffer theological disrepute. Resultantly, many Bible students, rather than risk such a trap, altogether avoid a study of this wicked person. They overlook the fact that Jesus himself instructed us to explore the book of Daniel for an understanding of the Antichrist.

When Jesus was explaining the signs of His second coming to the disciples, He noted that previous to His second advent, men would "see the abomination of desolation, spoken of by Daniel the prophet, stand in the holy place, (whoso readeth, let him understand)" (Matt. 24:15). Therefore, we are not turning to Daniel on some random hunch but, rather, in obedience to Jesus. We want to discover this man, who abominates and makes desolate and declares himself God, standing at the altar in God's re-

stored temple. He is described in Daniel 7:8,
24-27; 8:8, 9, 23-25; 9:26, 27; 12:11; and in the
greatest detail in 11:36-45. His empire is also described in Daniel 2.

The Antichrist will be a man who makes his
debut with nearly irresistible charm. He is soon
vested with an overpowering charisma—a character "of terrible countenance."

The wife of a prominent Torontian recounted
a dream she had recently of the Antichrist; he
was fascinating, strikingly handsome, and was
as alluring as a flame to a moth. He will appear
as an "angel" of peace, but become the most
cruel and ruthless warmonger of all time. He will
weave his hypnotic spell at first over a nation,
then ten nations, then the nerve center of the
earth—the Middle East—then over the Communist empire (which until then professes to believe in neither God nor devil), then the whole
world.

Among those who listened carefully to Jesus'
words was the Apostle John. After Pentecost, he
spent an entire generation, not only preaching
the Gospel, but probably reading and re-reading
the book of Daniel, as Jesus said he should. Late
in his life, on the Isle of Patmos, he received visions from Christ, and consequently wrote the
Book of the Revelation. In four of the five New
Testament books John wrote, he refers to the
coming Antichrist. In two of his three epistles,
he actually uses the term "antichrist."

Can any of us accurately identify the Antichrist at this time? Of course not. No more can we name him than we can specify the day and hour in which Christ will return. In 2 Thessalonians 2:7, 8, we are informed that the Holy Spirit presently restrains rampant iniquity; the Spirit will eventually be removed from the world, along with Christ's Church, "and then shall that Wicked be revealed." For all we know, the Antichrist is alive today—and may even be a grown man.

More significant than the unveiling of the Antichrist will be God's rescue of all true Christians from this tortured earth. That will be what theologians through the centuries have called the "rapture"—the "parousia"—literally, "the snatching away" of the Church. The Apostle Paul assures:

> For God hath not appointed us to wrath, but to obtain salvation by our Lord Jesus Christ, who died for us, that, whether we wake or sleep, we should live together with him. (1 Thess. 5:9, 10)

John was also writing of the "snatching away" when he quoted Jesus' words, "I will keep thee from the hour of temptation which shall come upon all the world. Behold, I come quickly" (Rev. 3:10,11). All true believers, of every century and country, will be caught up into the air to be with Jesus. There, in grand festivity, we will celebrate His redemption with the saints of all the ages.

But not all people will have this privilege.

Jesus said, "I tell you, in that night there shall be two men in one bed; one will be taken and the other shall be left. Two women shall be grinding together; the one shall be taken and the other left" (Luke 17:34, 35). We are to be ready, for at a time that we "think not," Jesus will come to claim His own.

Once Jesus has removed His Church from the earth, the Antichrist will identify himself unmistakeably by his relationship with Israel. He will make the most widely publicized peace agreement in the history of the world, guaranteeing Israel protection and freedom to worship in the restored ancient traditions of the Old Testament.

> And he shall confirm the covenant with many for one week: and in the midst of the week he shall cause the sacrifice and the oblation to cease, and for the overspreading of abominations he shall make it desolate, even until the consummation, and that determined shall be poured upon the desolate. (Dan. 9:27)

A study of these passages in Daniel provides the key to the length of time between Christ's rapture of the saints and His coming to earth to reign. The last half of the Antichrist's dominion is set by Daniel at three-and-a-half years, so that Antichrist will be operating approximately seven years after his manifestation. "And from the time that the daily sacrifice shall be taken away, and the abomination that maketh desolate set up, there shall be a thousand two hundred and ninety days" (Dan. 12:11). In Revelation, John says it is 42 months.

I believe Jesus was referring to Israel's acceptance of the Antichrist when He reproached the Jews, saying, "I am come in my Father's name, and ye receive me not: if another shall come in his own name, him ye will receive" (John 5:43).

The most obvious fulfillment of biblical prophecy in terms of the last days timetable is the return of Israel to their ancient homeland and the restoration of the country from desert to lush garden. No theme today gets more media attention than Israel's quest for peace and security. A glance at a current copy of The *Toronto Star* reveals four of six articles on the World News page centering on Israel. The subject is carried in seven of the twenty letters to the editor, and the leading editorial addresses the Soviet's current hardening against Zionism, as "once again . . . almost overnight, repression has been renewed with the arrest and intimidation of dissidents and a concerted effort to return to 'Stalin Terror.' "

The centripetal point for the increase of international tension, and finally World War III, will be a revived and restored Israel, of which we are currently seeing the initial stages. The tension was witnessed throughout 1980, when the matter of whether Jerusalem was merely the "de facto" or the "de june" Capital of Israel was hot-

ly discussed. Anwar Sadat threatened breaking
off relations with Israel if the Knesset declared
Jerusalem the "de june" (by law) capital. But
the Israeli Parliament went ahead and voted; an
"overwhelming majority" contended, along with
Prime Minister Begin, that Jerusalem is the
capital of Israel, "indivisible and forever!" This
is a landmark event in the fulfillment of prophecy, for Jews and for Christians.

Emil Fackenheim, Professor of Philosophy at
the University of Toronto, and author of such
books as *The Jewish Return Into History: Re-
flections in the Age of Auschwitz and a New Jerusalem,* commented that Jerusalem's being
proclaimed the "de june" capital of Israel is not
only a political but an eternal milestone for all
Jewish people. "What is the bond between Jerusalem and the Jewish people? And why is it," he
asks, that "no Israeli, 'hawk' or 'dove,' religious
or secular, pro- or anti-Begin, is prepared to give
up Jerusalem or have her redivided?" It is, he
answers himself, because the eternal "destiny of
Jerusalem and that of the Jewish people are
inseparable."

On August 22, 1980, the World Council of
Churches voiced official "opposition" to the Israeli "unilateral action of annexing East Jerusalem and uniting the city as its eternal capital under its exclusive sovereignty." The International
Jewish Committee on Interreligious Consulta-
tions countered immediately that, while others

General view of Jerusalem. United Nations Photo.

may have vital interests in Jerusalem, both historic and future, "for Jews only has it been the Eternal City, the center of their spiritual world and the focus of hope for millennia."

Jews are euphoric about returning to their homeland. Jacob Timerman, an Argentine newspaperman who has focused on building a new life in Israel, told *Newsweek* that it is the one place a Jew can be truly free. "If I had gone to the United States, my first act would have been to beg refuge," he said. "But in Israel, I did not have to ask for anything. The first thing said when I got off the plane was, 'Welcome Home!' "

President Reagan emphasizes that he believes, along with today's mainstream of Bible-believing Christians, that we in the West have no choice other than to support Israel's struggle for peace and provision, if we take seriously the teachings of Scripture. Consequently, the U.S. annually gives more aid to Israel (5 billion dollars) than to the rest of the world combined (4½ billion dollars), while trying to perform a deadly balancing act with the Arabs, since 40% of U.S. oil supplies are currently imported.

Prime Minister Begin insisted that Israel's greatest unending challenge is the achievement of peace and security. The "pressure" and the "price" of it, he admits, is becoming almost unbearable for the Jewish People. So when the Antichrist offers the Israelis, who are desperate for peace, a guarantee of security, it will be welcomed with open arms. Israelis are longing for "a veritable miracle, or savior, to provide immediate relief."

When British commentator James Cameron returned from talks with Israeli leaders in 1980, he was particularly impressed by one fact: they wanted peace and security above all else. They must have their borders guaranteed. They have lost confidence in the United Nations. If a strongman with enough clout to guarantee peace would arise, Cameron maintained, they would "accept that man and give him almost anything he wants." That man, of course, is on the way!

What will be the empire of the Antichrist? Most encyclopedias, Protestant or Catholic, indicate that it will initially coincide with the ancient Roman Empire; this view is based on Daniel 2 and 7, and Revelation 13 and 17. This would constitute a bloc of ten western nations. As we concluded previously, the completion of the Common Market goal of ten-member nations is noteworthy in light of this prophecy. *Time* commented, "When the EC expanded from six to nine countries" (and now to ten), Europe had achieved her "greatest unity since the beginning of the breakup of Charlemagne's Empire in 814." Greece's entry into the EC in January, 1981, completes the ten.

It is not my view, however, that the ten-nation confederacy will be restricted to the confines of the ancient Roman Empire. It's dominion will, I expect, go far beyond these boundaries, since the Antichrist's empire is to be a world power (Rev. 13:8).

In Revelation 17:1-7, the woman arrayed in purple and scarlet is seen sitting upon a scarlet-colored beast. I see this woman as apostate Christendom, those who reject Christ, and the beast as the Antichrist and his empire. Christ loves the Church and gave himself for it. But when He comes to "rapture" His saints, He will take only His true Church home, whether its individuals are from the Catholic, Protestant, Orthodox, Jewish, or another religious group and the Bible is very clear concerning the fact that the true Church is made up of those who have personally received Jesus Christ as their Lord and Saviour, the true Messiah.

I personally do not believe that the United States will play a crucial role in Bible prophecy, even though it holds such a significant position in the current political/economic scene. When my American brothers ask me why, I point to the recent statistics. A Gallup poll indicates that seventy million (52%) adult Americans profess to be "born again." What would happen to the U.S. if all those people, along with millions of small children who have not yet reached an age of accountability, were suddenly taken up out of the earth?

Look at the leadership of the U.S. All three of

the main candidates for the Presidency in 1980 openly claimed to be "born again," and were attempting daily to read the Scriptures and walk with Christ. Six of the last seven Presidents claimed to be "born again." (Whether they were or not is God's decision; we don't keep the books: "The Lord knoweth them that are his"—2 Tim. 2:19.)

Just as animals in the jungle rush together for mutual consolation at the roar of the big beast, so the unbelieving, unregenerate church members of the world will rush together and mount the beast's "bandwagon" once the true believers are gone. This is what Paul was writing about in 2 Thessalonians 2:8-12:

> And then shall that Wicked be revealed . . . even him, whose coming is after the working of Satan with all power and signs and lying wonders, and with all deceivableness of unrighteousness in them that perish; because they received not the love of the truth, that they might be saved. And for this cause God shall send them strong delusion, that they should believe a lie: that they all might be damned who believed not the truth, but had pleasure in unrighteousness.

There will be a coming together of millions of Protestant and Catholic "nominal" members, who are left behind when Christ comes again. They will no doubt be joined by many other religionists as well. There seemed to be a preview of the ecclesiastical "shape of things to come" when, in 1979, leaders of the ten major religions of the world met in New Jersey. In that conference, Christians, Buddhists, Confucianists, Hindus, Jews, Janists, Muslims, Sikhs, Shintoists and Zoroastrians jointly issued their "Princeton Declaration of the World Conference on Religion and Peace." Such a religious amalgam will no doubt be in existence as the Antichrist establishes his empire, and the false prophet can quickly seize control of the organization. (I have no intention of questioning the motives of those who conceived this conference at Princeton.)

Though the chronology of events is not yet clear, it appears that the next major episode, after the Antichrist emerges as the leader in the West and the Middle East, will be a large-scale war. The armies of Gog, the land of Magog (possibly Russia), will be destroyed as they attempt to descend on Israel (Ezekiel 38, 39). This will be the first terrible apocalyptical event early in the "Great Tribulation."

Ezekiel 38 and 39 deal with the restoration of Israel to its ancient homeland, its anguished struggle for peace, and its dread of the eventual conflict which nearly every observer recognizes as inevitable. When David Ben Gurion made the establishing Proclamation of Israel as a nation in May, 1948, he read to the world, over the radio, from Ezekiel.

The 38th chapter of Ezekiel begins:

> And the word of the Lord came unto me,

saying, Son of man, set thy face against Gog, the land of Magog, the chief prince of Meshech and Tubal, and prophesy against him, and say, Thus saith the Lord God; Behold, I am against thee, O Gog, the chief prince of Meshech and Tubal. (Ezek. 38:1-3)

Verse 2 of the above passage seems to be the key verse. The word "man" is translated from "adam" and is a generic term referring to mankind. The word "set" is *siym* and means to put or place something with a sense of determination. The Hebrew *el* is here translated "against," and signifies action toward someone or something. God is thus saying to the son of mankind that he should determinedly place his face toward Gog.

"Gog," related to Meshech and Tubal as their chief prince, may be a head prince such as Beelzebub, mentioned in the New Testament. It is conceivable that Gog is a chief prince (Heb. *rosh*—head of principal authority; Heb. *nasee*—one who is exalted or lifted up) among the fallen angels or evil spirits in the same manner that Michael is a principal and exalted angel in the Kingdom of God. In Daniel 10:13, 20, the prince of Persia and the prince of Grecia seem to be in the fallen or evil spirit category. If they had been mere men, it would not have taken two chief angels—Michael and Gabriel—to withstand them. It therefore seems possible that Gog is the evil spirit that will impel the vast northern armies toward the land of Israel in the latter days.

Magog was a son of Japheth and a grandson of Noah. Josephus, a Jewish historian, noted that the Greeks called the descendants of Magog Scythians. The Scythians settled north of Mt. Ararat, which is in the southern Caucasus, in the province of Georgia, Russia.

Meshech was a brother to Magog. His name is derived from the Hebrew prime root *mashak*, meaning to draw out. The descendants of Meshech were reputedly a barbarous people who inhabited the Moschian Mountains, between Iberia, Armenia, and Colchis.

Tubal was another son of Japheth. According to some scholars, his descendants were sometimes called the Tibareni, a nation of Asia Minor, dwelling by the Black Sea to the west of "Meshech." If historians are accurate, then the descendants of the two brothers Tubal and Meshech inhabit adjoining territories in southern Russia, between the Black and the Caspian Seas.

Ezekiel was admonished by God to prophesy (Heb. *navay*—to speak by divine power) against Gog and his northern hordes. Many Bible commentators feel that Russia is the major northern nation that will move in the spirit of Gog to destroy Israel. The Jews refer to this confrontation as the battle of Gog-Magog.

The Babylonian Talmud states: " . . . but

when the battle of Gog-Magog will come about they will ask, 'For what purpose have you come?' And they will reply: 'Against God and His Messiah' " (Abodah Zarah, pp. 8-9). This will be another attempt by Satan (the name literally means hinder or adversary) to foil the plan of God. If he could destroy Israel, Messiah would no longer be necessary and the integrity of God's Word would therefore be suspect. Satan knows he cannot win in a direct confrontation with God, but he will do all he can to damage God's integrity by thwarting the completion of His covenant with the Jewish people.

Gog, a high, principal authority of the satanic kingdom, is preparing his strategy against the "apple [Heb. *iyshon*—pupil] of God's eye," Jacob or Israel. In Ezekiel 38:4, the phrase "turn thee back" comes from the Hebrew prime root *shoov* which means to turn about. The word "hooks" is translated from *khakheem* and indicates a ring which is clasped to an animal's nose or lip, for the purpose of leading about. "Jaws" is translated from the unused root *lekhiy* and denotes the cheek because of its fleshiness. The statement "I will bring thee forth" is *hotsatee*, from the root *yatsa*, meaning "to bring out or cause to go forth." Thus Jehovah is saying to the kingdom of the north, "I will turn you about-face, put a ring in your cheek, and cause you to go forth to battle."

Ezekiel 38:5 reveals the names of three people or nations that will accompany the northern invaders against Israel: Persia (modern Iran), Ethiopia and Libya. In a recent CBC interview, Anwar Sadat noted that Iran, Ethiopia and Libya are seemingly full allies with the Soviets. Until recently, Iran was firmly established in the Western camp. The change to new government was swift, as a *London Daily Telegraph* headline announced, "Iran's 2,500 Years of Monarchy Ends in Twenty Minutes." The overthrow of the Shah and the establishment of a Muslim government, which has resulted in national chaos, seems to open the way for ancient Persia to become allied with Russia. Even though the fanatic Muslims and the atheistic Soviets have no apparent ideological grounds for compatibility, their mutual animosity toward the Jews could easily provide a basis for fraternity.

Iran is presently full of unrest and confusion. Neither the economy nor the political leadership has stabilized, and it seems the youth are disenchanted with the Ayatollah Khomeini who is in ill health. Such turmoil could easily lead to another change in government—especially a pro-Soviet administration. The Soviet Union shares part of its southern border with Iran, and since its invasion of Afghanistan in 1979, it also occupies Iran's eastern border. An alliance between the two countries could bring a military staging area even closer to the land of Israel.

After the incredibly bungled attempt to

retrieve the American hostages in Iran, Joseph Kraft wrote under the headline, "Russians Are the Big Winners," that "the abortive American effort to rescue the hostages drove Iran into a frenzy of hatred." If there were now an international showdown, there's no doubt that Iran would join the Soviets to bring down the Americans, especially if the conflict involved Israel.

Mark Gayn, in a 1980 editorial, notes that "the Soviets are pushing southward," having already brought Ethiopia "under their control." Since Emperor Haile Selassie's death, Ethiopia has rapidly joined hands with the Soviets. It almost reads as though they are already mobilizing for their future role in Bible prophecy. A 1980 Reuter report revealed that Ethiopia's 40,000 government troops "supported by Soviet tanks, artillery and aircraft" are already making northward moves.

Then, of course, there is Libya, which threw its support behind Iraq in the Iraq-Iran war of 1980. "Is Qaddafi a Madman?" a *Toronto Star* headline asked in 1980. The media coverage Colonel Muammar Qaddafi has garnered shows him firmly allied with the Soviets. This was further strengthened when Syria, a longtime Russian ally, "united" with Libya to become one country.

An article in *Time* pointed to Libya, Iran, and Ethiopia—with its strategic location on the Horn of Africa—as the Soviet's three prize plumbs of the last five years. This seems to point strongly to the prophecy in Ezekiel 38.

In 38:6 we are told that "Gomer, and all his bands" and "the house of Togarmah of the north quarters" will also participate in the attack on Israel. Gomer was the firstborn of Japheth, son of Noah. The name Gomer is derived from the Hebrew prime root *gamar,* meaning "to end." Gomer is usually identified with the "Gimiraa" in the Assyrian, and the "Kimmeioi" in the Greek (*Encyclopedia Judaica*, Vol. U, p. 768). There is some indication that the descendants of Gomer settled in three areas: in Eastern Europe, on the British Isles (the Celtics), and north of the Caspian Sea in Russia (*The Chronology of the Bible*, Frank R. Klassen, p. 9).

Gomer had a son named Ashkenaz, whose descendants are considered to be part of the Germanic peoples (*Bible Dictionary*, Ehud Ben-Yehuda/David Weinstein, p. 129). Ashkenaz is not mentioned in Ezekiel.

Togarmah was also a son of Gomer. The Armenians regard Torgam (the same as Togarmah), the son of Gomer, as the founder of their nation, and call themselves "The House of Torgam" (*Hebrew and Chaldee Lexicon,* Gesenius, p. 856). Also, Torgamah was probably the ancient name of Armenia (*Bible Dictionary,* William Smith, p. 705). Armenia is located near the eastern border of Turkey.

Ezekiel 38:7 admonishes Gog and all his company (Heb. *kahal*—congregation) to be prepared (Heb. *koon*—prime root "to be erect," hence, "set up") and to be a guard (Heb. *mishmar*—to have custody as a watchman, from prime root *shamar*—to hedge about). Thus Gog is to set up a multi-national congregation of warriors, over which he has custody, and ready them for an attack.

From this point (Ezek. 38:8-39:29) we witness one of the most gruesome accounts in all literature, as God foretells the converging of enemy nations against Israel "in the latter years." As I interpret the prophetic timetable, this will take place at the midpoint of the tribulation, while Antichrist's treaty with Israel is still in effect. Therefore, I believe Antichrist will side with Israel at this time. The invaders will be brutally defeated; the account speaks of pestilence, blood, flood, hail, fire, and brimstone.

It is my view that somehow, during this holocaust, the Antichrist will die, descend into perdition, and rise from the dead. Consolidating his hold in Jerusalem and with a second beast, the false prophet, at his side, he will rally his forces to conquer the world, over which he will rule for only a short time. A communique from the Club of Rome warns, "Crises lead to war, and war today means nuclear conflagration, which in turn spells collective suicide. . . . Only a global plan . . . can avert universal catastrophe." The Antichrist will offer that global plan, and the world, seeing itself disintegrating into anarchy and chaos, will gladly accept it.

Seeing a title like James Burnham's *Suicide of the West*, many people ask, "Will nuclear war, which can in a matter of minutes wipe out half the world's population, be avoidable?" If my interpretation of Revelation 6-19 is correct, the answer is no. A recent article in *Time* entitled, "To the Brink and Back 330 Times," claims there have been 330 occasions (10% of them perilously close to the precipice) since World War II that the U.S. and the U.S.S.R. have approached possible nuclear conflict. The article concludes that history places the odds against man's capacity to avoid such a war indefinitely.

Man will not be able to save himself from war because the Antichrist, empowered directly by Satan, will be history's greatest man of war (Rev. 13:4). Man will at first "wonder" after the beast, but will eventually be possessed by him.

Satan is no longer an obscure, ridiculous figure of mythology in our society; people have become inordinately conscious of him. A glance at current bookstands is revealing and frightening. There are scores of books on Satan, or using his name. *The Devil's Alternative* was a large seller in 1980. Other titles on the market include *Devil's Brand, Devil's Bride, Devil's Desire, Devil's Handmaidens, Devil's House, Devil's Own, Devil's Piper,* and *Devil's Virtuoso*. Man will indeed find himself "between the devil and the deep blue sea."

When Billy Graham was in England in 1980,

he commented after a trip to London, "I counted 19 movie pictures that had to do with the occult and the devil." Films reflect our society. And this obsession with the devil indicates that people are aware of the forces of evil that are rapidly gathering momentum for a final crescendo of iniquity.

Today, it is not the Bible-wavers who can be accused as wholesalers of gloom and doom. It is, instead, the media which is waving the black flags. For example, in mid-1980, the *Edmonton Sun* carried an article pointing to 1982. That's the year the planets align themselves behind the sun and astrologists and psychics are saying the rare solar event will cause tremendous gravitational pull on the earth and result in cataclysmic upheavals." Because of Jesus' clear instructions, the Bible-believer does not name dates. However, he does, with God-given understanding, look on future events as precursing the rise of the Antichrist, and ultimately, the return of Jesus Christ.

Chapter Seven

*"The abomination of desolation, spoken of by
Daniel the prophet" (Matt. 24:15).*

Carlyle once noted that "the history of a people is the biography of its great men." To study
history is to study the people who made things
happen—people who were responsible for events
which affected the direction that humanity has
traveled, from creation to the present. Therefore
a study of the first generation A.D. requires a
look at the life of Jesus Christ; a study of the
early nineteenth century requires a look at Napoleon; and a study of the 1930s and 1940s neces-
sitates a look at Hitler.

A study of the seven-year period of tribulation on earth, subsequent to Christ's rapture of
the saints, is largely a look at the life and times
of the Antichrist. In the Bible, the Antichrist is
called by many names (even as 365 names are
ascribed to our Lord). In Daniel 9:26, he is referred to as "the prince." This, of course, implies
that people will be under his rule.

Jesus, referring to the Antichrist, called him
"the abomination of desolation"—"When ye

therefore shall see the abomination of desolation, spoken of by Daniel the prophet, stand in the holy place (whoso readeth, let him understand)" (Matt. 24:15). In the previous chapter, when we discussed Daniel 9:27 for the purpose of chronology, this meant: "He shall cause the sacrifice and the oblation to cease, and for the overspreading of abominations he shall make it desolate. . . . " This is what Jesus alluded to when He said, "Then there will be great tribulation" (Matt. 24:21).

Daniel, of course, predicted a near and a far desolation of the Jewish temple, the near being fulfilled when Antiochus Epiphanes offered slaughtered pigs on the Jewish temple altar. That act was already history when Jesus spoke, so there must be another and further fulfillment yet to come.

The Apostle Paul informed the Thessalonians that the Antichrist, the "man of sin," would be "revealed, the son of perdition; who opposeth and exalteth himself above all that is called God, or that is worshipped; so that he as God sitteth in the temple of God, shewing himself that he is God" (2 Thess. 2:3, 4). This raises the question, "Does the temple have to be rebuilt in Jerusalem by the time God's timetable reaches the mid-point of the tribulation?" I am convinced that a new temple is an absolute necessity for the completion of the prophetic picture.

Orthodox Jews have longed for the rebuilding

of the temple of Jerusalem. Several years ago a huge advertisement appeared in the *Washington Post*, announcing, "To persons of the Jewish faith all over the world, a project to rebuild the Temple of God in Israel is now being started. With Divine guidance and help the Temple of God is now being started. . . . God will know those desiring to participate." A box number was included.

Late in 1979 I was riding in Indiana with a local Presbyterian minister. At a certain point along the highway he informed me that we were driving past the gate of a company which purportedly handled a highly classified order of the finest building stones in the world. Sixty thousand tons of pre-cut stones had been shipped on 500 rail cars. They were allegedly bought by the Israeli Government, and had already arrived in Israel.

It has been reported that young men from the tribe of Levi are being trained for temple service, including the offering of animal sacrifices. This would assure that priests will be ready in the event the Temple is completed.

But how can the Temple be erected when the Al Aqsa Mosque (Dome of the Rock), the third most sacred Muslim shrine, is standing on the supposed site of Solomon's Temple? There are various possibilities. For instance, a natural disaster, such as an earthquake, might handily destroy the structure.

Another possible means would be by human

destruction. In 1980, a group of Orthodox Jewish zealots plotted to blow up the Al Aqsa Mosque, in observance of the thirteenth anniversary of the reunification of Jerusalem. The international repercussions of such a demolition could have been disastrous. Fortunately, the scheme was foiled before it succeeded.

A third possibility is that the original Temple site may actually be in another spot. In the *Jewish Chronicle* (March 28, 1980), it was reported that a Hebrew University physicist, Dr. Asher Kaufman, "has broken with tradition to place the Temple about fifty metres north of the Dome of the Rock." Kaufman's controversial theory is based on a study of "written sources, particularly the Mishna (the Jewish oral tradition, finally redacted in A.D. 220), his own archaeological observations and complicated scientific calculations." The physicist seems sure "that the foundation stone is the bedrock floor beneath a cupola at the northwestern end of the Temple Mount, known as the Dome of the Spirits or Dome of the Tablets."

Whatever the solution to the dilemma, the Temple of Solomon will be rebuilt. And not too many years after its completion, it would seem, the Antichrist will be sitting, "as God sitteth in the temple of God, shewing himself that he is God." In Daniel 11:36-38, we read of the Antichrist:

> And the king shall do according to his will; and he shall exalt himself, and magnify him-

Dome of the Rock, Jerusalem. United Nations photo.

self above every god, and shall speak marvellous things against the God of gods, and shall prosper till the indignation be accomplished: for that that is determined shall be done. Neither shall he regard the God of his fathers, nor the desire of women, nor regard any god: for he shall magnify himself above all. But in his estate shall he honour the God of forces: and a god whom his fathers knew not shall he honour with gold, and silver, and with precious stones, and pleasant things.

How a man can exalt himself as God, and be acknowledged as such, seems absurd in our "enlightened" age; but it is not at all impossible, even among atheistic people. A *Boston Sun* reporter noted that the Soviet hierarchy twice annually stand before Lenin's preserved remains and worshipfully exclaim, "Glory! Glory! Glory!"

One of the Antichrist's accomplishments will be to unify the currency and establish some system of fund transfer that will probably eliminate the use of cash: "And he causeth all . . . to receive a mark in their right hand, or in their foreheads: and that no man might buy or sell, save he that had the mark, or the name of the beast, or the number of his name" (Rev. 13:16, 17).

The U.S. system of Social Security numbers demonstrates the viability of such a system. In Holland, every newborn baby is automatically assigned a number. Also, a process has now been developed whereby a number can be imprinted invisibly on a person's hand or forehead by an electronic device, and can be read instantly by a scanning instrument. The Antichrist may not necessarily use such methods, but they obviously show that the numbering and marking process can easily be implemented.

In this regard, I have often been asked about the highly secretive Trilateral Commission, which was initiated by David Rockefeller, and includes financiers, intellectuals and heads of governments in eight Western European nations, Japan, and the U.S. The Commission is committed to the development of one-world government, one-world bank, and one-world currency.

An article in the *London Daily Mirror* referred to the core members of the Commission as "Kingmakers," and noted that:

> One of the most remarkable successes of the Trilateral Commission was the election of Jimmy Carter as U.S. President in 1976. It was during lunch in London in the autumn of 1972 that Rockefeller decided to help the presidential aspirations of the unknown Jimmy Carter. He invited Carter to join the Commission. Carter leapt at the chance.
>
> But most astonishing of all, once Carter was elected he chose almost his entire Cabinet from the sixty-three original American members of the Trilateral Commission, including Zbigniew Brzezinski, Cyrus Vance, Walter Mondale, Harold Brown, Michael Blumenthal and Andrew Young.

The members of the Trilateral Commission

keep their activities exceedingly confidential, but there is no doubt that while they don't talk loudly, they carry a very big stick. Their intentions are probably good, but it is possible that they may be a part of the eventual weaving of the Antichrist's web.

The European Common Market is much more visible and vocal regarding the trend toward a universal money system. For example, Britain and Ireland, both strongly traditional, switched their currencies to the decimal system after joining the EC. In another instance, *Time* notes, "One month after the latest monetary crisis, Cabinet officers, legislators and bankers on both sides of the Atlantic are intensely debating a lengthening list of ideas" for developing "a global financial system." Bank America is currently using an advertising campaign which announces, "The whole world welcomes world money."

Bible scholars have for decades been predicting this development in the international economic system. And as this evolves, there is surfacing a rash of methods which eliminate the need for cash and personal handling of money. Canada's Minister of Finance reckons that we are moving quickly to a system where credit card use will be replaced by a bank-operated, electronic-payment system. A *Reader's Digest* article entitled, "Coming Soon: Electronic Money," claimed that millions of Americans are already receiving their wages and salaries electronically,

with bank deposits, loan payments, and out-
standing bills automatically processed.

"In his estate shall he honour the God of
forces" (Dan. 11:38). Though he'll eventually be
responsible for the most devastating war in human history, the Antichrist's initial appeal will
partially center around a promise to restore "law
and order." This will come at a time when the
world is reeling with anarchistic guerrilla terror-
ism and rampant crime. Crime is already on the
increase, worldwide. FBI Director William H.
Webster reported that crime in North America
rose an unbelievable 10% during 1980. Dr. Alfred
Messer, chief of psychiatry at Atlanta's North-
side Hospital, projects that "crime will continue
to increase as in net restraints on behavior are
weakened. . . . With the decline of religion, with
the decline of tradition, with the loss of family
structure . . . the crime rate is headed for dou-
ble-digit figures."

North America is not the only place this is
occurring. Even the Russians cannot control this
problem. A Soviet magazine, *Kaya Rossiya*,
states that Russian sociologists and law-enforce-
ment officers lament "an alarming rise in juve-
nile crime." We can be sure that when the Antichrist comes, pledging the kind of force
necessary to repress such disorder, his offer will
have broad appeal.

If the Antichrist "shall honour the God of
forces," he will no doubt be a militarist, in the

vein of the late Mao Tse-tung, who said that nothing is useful which does not come out of the barrel of a cannon. Of course, Mao had to kill an estimated 100 million dissidents in order to subjugate a fifth of the human race. Somehow he will exhibit enough power to enforce his rule. This could be done by means of thermonuclear devices or possibly some other means yet undiscovered. The Scriptures do say that "he doeth great wonders, so that he maketh fire come down from heaven on the earth in the sight of men" (Rev. 13:13). Such phenomenon could also be possible through other means, such as one exhibited at the 1976 Olympics: the Olympic flame in Montreal was ignited by a laser beam aimed via satellite from the ancient Olympic site in Greece.

As I read an editorial in the *Toronto Star* in late 1980, I could not help but think of how the Antichrist "shall honour the God of forces." The editorial was assessing the horrifying military weapons at man's disposal:

> [The world] has whole arsenals of nuclear weapons large enough to destroy every man, woman and child five times over. We have weapons to vaporize cities and their populations, to flatten mountains and turn forests into fire storms. We have weapons that kill people without damaging buildings. We can kill quickly, with a big bang, or slowly, with silent and insidious radiation.

And now there is a new "escalation of the development and production of deadly gasses and germ-laden bombs that would turn air, water and vegetation into an invading army."

One of the "gods" the Antichrist will engage and maximize is the god of "science"—not only physical science, but biophysical science. Pope John Paul II, addressing the United Nations Educational, Scientific and Cultural Organization (UNESCO), implored man to abolish the suicidal perils of "chemical, bacteriological and nuclear" weaponry. Then turning to the subject of "genetical manipulations in biological experiments," he pleaded that men maintain "the priority of the ethical over the technical, of the primacy of human being over things, of the superiority of the spirit over matter."

India's Prime Minister Indira Gandhi, in her address to the Global Conference on the Future in Toronto, asserted, "The discoveries of molecular biology and also the development of weapons of destruction have almost obliterated the line between life and non-life."

Riding the wave of this progress, the Antichrist will exploit these terrible potentialities of science to further his own schemes. Here again is why the true Christ *must* come and subdue him.

We learn in Revelation 13:16 that the Antichrist will have in his domain, "great and small, rich and poor." Thus we can be sure that in the time of the Great Tribulation there will be an ironic inequity in society, with the wealthy reclining in luxury. Revelation 17 and 18 describe the Babylonian indulgences in which men live for greed, gluttony, drunkenness, and immorality.

Max Lerner has said that the current North American life-style is a Babylonian existence. Columnist Tom Harper claims that in America, 65% of the food in restaurants and 25% of the food in our homes is wasted. In 1980, North Americans bought pills, liquid protein, sweat girdles, and exercise equipment in order to get off the fat, at an expense of 12 billion dollars—more than the total national budget of the world's wealthiest-per-capita nation (outside the Arab world), Switzerland! In the midst of such extravagance, the World Health Organization projects that one billion people will die from famine during the 1980s—Jesus said that during the last days there would be "famines . . . in divers places." (Interestingly, the third-world nations which are suffering such rampant hunger are spending five times more on armaments than on agricultural machinery—swords rather than plowshares.)

The most conspicuous characteristics of the Antichrist will be his terrible "wrath" and "anger," and total dedication (despite his initial talk of peace) to all-out war. He will usher in the "great tribulation, such as was not since the beginning of the world to this time, no, nor ever shall be. And except those days should be shortened, there should no flesh be saved" (Matt. 24:21, 22).

Times under the Antichrist's reign will become increasingly worse. They will go from chaos to iron-handed terror; from rumors of war to Armageddon. Man will be sliding to the brink of annihilation, "but for the elect's sake those days shall be shortened" (Matt. 24:22). Christ will come in glory with the holy angels and the saints of the ages to inaugurate a reign of peace and plenty for a thousand years.

The recent holocaust in Cambodia is a sort of microcosm of the global horrors of the Great Tribulation. All the gruesome aspects are there: cold-blooded persecution, war, pestilence and famine. In seven years, the *New York Times* claims, 3.4 million have died from murder, war, and starvation, leaving 5.5 million to face chronic despair and genocide.

The seven-year period of the Great Tribulation will be similar, if multiplied by a thousand times. One of the great tormentors during this time will be "BABYLON THE GREAT, THE MOTHER OF HARLOTS AND ABOMINATIONS OF THE EARTH" (Rev. 17:5). She will be on the rampage against all true believers, and will be "drunken with the blood of the saints, and with the blood of the martyrs of Jesus" (Rev. 17:6). Religious or economic freedom will be nonexistent at this time.

But would people relinquish economic authority to a dictator? When it comes to the economy, people at present are desperate. A *Los Angeles Times* survey indicates that 68% of Americans feel that the United States is in an "economic emergency *more dangerous* than any military threat from abroad." This accounts for why Howard Ruff's *How to Prosper During the Coming Bad Years* is a bestseller, and why Willard Cantelon's *The Day the Dollar Died* gains such wide readership.

I believe that the coming Great Tribulation is a product of Satan's wrath, not God's. It appears to me that Satan precipitates the Tribulation by venting his anger on the human race: "Woe to the inhabiters of the earth and of the sea! for the devil is come down unto you, having great wrath, because he knoweth that he hath but a short time" (Rev. 12:12).

Columnist Max Rafferty wrote in 1980 that Satanism and witchcraft, even now, are cutting a terrifyingly wide swath across the activities of young Americans. The devil is already entrenching himself. The horrors of the Tribulation will be deliberate, inspired by Satan, in a manner previewed for us in the atrocities perpetrated by the Pol Pot regime. The tortures and the butcher-like executions of suspected enemies all bear the marks of demonic cruelty.

The biblical timetable of end-time events is made clear in Revelation 6. As I see it, war, famine and pestilence (Rev. 6:1-8) all occur before the actual Great Tribulation itself: "And when he had opened the fifth seal, I saw under the altar the souls of them that were slain for the word of God" (Rev. 6:9). But all will not be lost during Antichrist's reign. God will still be enthroned in heaven, and working mightily on earth. According to Revelation 14:6, an angel will "fly in the midst of heaven, having the everlasting gospel to preach unto them that dwell on the earth, and to every nation, and kindred, and tongue, and people." John recorded that those who answer the call to Christ would be "a great multitude, which no man could number" (Rev. 7:9).

The main reason Antichrist will impose his "mark of the beast" is to try to stamp out worshipers of Jesus. If he cannot kill them, they will, he expects, starve to death since they cannot buy or sell without the mark. The two most conspicuous victims of the Antichrist's persecution will be the "two witnesses" of Revelation 11. We read that all the people of the earth will see their corpses. How could this be? Or how could the whole world worship the image of the beast? Only in the last generation, through the development of television and satellite communication, has this become possible. Now, via satellite, a TV signal can be broadcast to any place in the world. And more and more people throughout the earth have TV sets. For example, in 1970 there was only one TV set for every 15,400 people in Mainland China. Today, the ratio is one for every 200, and by 1985, it will be one in 15.

"Technology," Billy Graham declared, will actually "hasten the appearance of the Antichrist, who will be seen worldwide on television." He is convinced that

> TV has to be linked with the Biblical prophecy [Rev. 11], that someday there will appear an Antichrist and the Antichrist will be seen by the whole world at the same time. People used to laugh at this passage—but that was before television was invented. But TV is only one of many indications that the Antichrist will be coming.

Cal Thomas, a veteran reporter, said on a television show that he believes the Antichrist will be a TV personality. By master-minding the media, he will draw the people's loyalty to himself. Whether or not Thomas is correct, TV will make it possible for the Antichrist to have his every move and every word monitored by cameramen and transmitted throughout the world.

It is obvious to anyone aware of the world scene that the technology for communication, data processing, and military weaponry is developing at blinding speed. Not only is the world ready for a leader in an economic, political, and spiritual sense, but now it is also technologically feasible for that person to step into power and carry out his purposes.

Chapter Eight

*"Whom the Lord shall consume with the spirit
of his mouth, and shall destroy with the brightness of his coming" (2 Thess. 2:8)*

The world under the satanic influence of the
Antichrist will be boiling with the turbulent
"great tribulation, such as was not since the beginning of the world to this time, no, nor ever
shall be" (Matt. 24:21). Mankind will have fall-
en to its absolute nadir. Nature itself will be in
convulsions. There will be signs in the sun, moon
and stars, and earthquakes everywhere. A reading of Revelation 4-19 boggles the mind with
images of apocalyptic destruction, when a third
of the world's population is destroyed, and then
half of what remains. Nothing will ever parallel
the awfulness of the wrath of Satan and the
wrath of God in conflict.

We have seen the vastness of destruction
from Mount St. Helens eruption. In the last five
years of the 1970s, more people were killed by
earthquakes than in the entire 75 years preced-
ing. In fact, 25 of the 49 largest earthquakes
in recorded history occurred from 1960 to
1980—only 2 decades!

But Revelation indicates that the worst earthquakes in history are still to come. Secular research is now providing the same foreboding. Doubleday's recent release, *Pole Shift*, by another John W. White and based on a theory of "the Jupiter Effect," is written from a strictly nonreligious, geophysical, and astrophysical viewpoint. If this "Jupiter Effect" occurs, beginning in 1982, the resulting earthquakes and volcanic explosions would cause widespread loss of life and severely affect weather through several growing seasons.

Here is the world situation projected by White:

> Imagine how much dust might be thrown into the atmosphere in a period of global volcanism. Sunlight would be reduced and temperatures would be lowered. Only the most cold-hardy or protected crops would survive and even they would be reduced in yield.
>
> The economic, political and social consequences of such a situation are clearly foreseeable. Massive starvation and skyrocketing inflation would lead to food riots and urban/suburban chaos. (The U.S. Dept. of Commerce estimates that food stores have at most, only a five-day supply of goods on hand if all shipments were halted.) Politically speaking, there would be a most unwelcome harvest—population relocation leading to international strife, which could well include nuclear warfare.
>
> Just as bad, these sorts of events would be strong confirmation of the longer-term predictions by psychics and prophets which say

there will be changes in the geography of our planet over the next two decades, ending with a cataclysmic pole shift in which the earth either tumbles suddenly in space or else slips its crust over the molten interior. This pole shift has been predicted for 1999 or 2000, and one source has identified the trigger mechanism as a rare near-grand alignment of the planets on May 5, 2000.

This projection is just that—a projection, not a prediction. I do not wish to press anyone's panic button, nor do I claim any special revelation. But an informal study of the eruption intervals of several major volcanoes was made by an engineer-friend of mine, with results that support this projection. He studied the data for Etna, Vesuvius, Pelee and Soufriere, and found that over the last 200 years, they all were increasing their frequency of eruption. When he projected his data, all lines converged in the 1982-84 period, leading him to conclude that the planet would enter a time of near-continuous eruptions then.

The geophysical and social cataclysms during the time of the Antichrist will climax in the battle of Armageddon. According to Daniel and the Apostle John, this will take place just prior to the second coming of Jesus Christ. As I understand it, though some scholars feel the time is longer, this will occur seven years after Christ comes to meet His Church in the air—the Rapture. The battle will be waged on the plain of Megiddo (also referred to as Armageddon and the Valley of Jehoshaphat), a 14-by-20-mile tract of land which Napoleon allegedly appraised as the ideal battleground. "Armageddon," according to the *New Catholic Encyclopedia*, "will be the place where antichrist will summon the kings of the earth for the final battle of mankind."

As I interpret prophecy, the Southern, Northern, and Eastern blocs of nations will all converge to engage the Antichrist and his forces, who basically will be the forces of "the West." Like any totalitarian dictator, the Antichrist will have to face a final showdown in an attempt to maintain his tyranny. Europe is already strongly aligned, divided between the West and the East. Africa is forming its own bloc of nations, known as The Organization of African Unity. In the Far East, China's Chairman Deng has projected that as Europe has its EC, so the Far East will have its Asian Community of Nations.

"And at the time of the end shall the king of the south push at him: and the king of the north shall come against him like a whirlwind, with chariots, and with horsemen" (Dan. 11:40). These are only some of the armies that march on Israel. The amount of people involved in this "finale" will be mind-boggling. Revelation 9:6 indicates that the armies from the east will number 200 million troops.

The prophet Joel announced:

> Proclaim ye this among the Gentiles; Prepare war, wake up the mighty men, let all the men of war draw near; let them come up: beat

your plowshares into swords, and your pruning hooks into spears. . . . Assemble yourselves, and come, all ye heathen, and gather yourselves together round about. . . . Let the heathen be wakened, and come up to the valley of Jeshoshaphat. (Joel 3:9-12)

But what overpowering evil could possess mankind to assemble for such a universal, and terminal, war? Very possibly, drug and alcohol abuse by the people of the world, and their rulers in particular could be a factor. The use of mind-bending substances has become an epidemic in the last decade. Marijuana is a 57-billion-dollar-a-year business—the third largest business in the U.S. A Toronto police officer lamented in mid-1980 that LSD use was up 50% in one year. Angel dust, glue, heroin—"You name it, and it's here—everywhere."

Los Angeles District Attorney John Van De Kamp has spoken of the "glorification of drugs, with syringes, capsules, coke kits, roach clips, bongs and power hitters becoming the new idols of millions of American youth." According to a Gallup poll, parents throughout the nation recognize that alcohol and drug use is on a "dramatic rise" and is "becoming one of the nation's most serious problems."

Two recent American Presidents each had a son named Jack. And both those sons caused great embarrassment to their families by having smoked pot.

According to the *New York Times*, in just one year in New York State, there has been a 46% increase in heroin-related hospital cases, and a 77% increase in deaths from use of the drug.

North America is not the only place with such problems. In fact, in the Soviet Union, the *Toronto Star* claims that "the average person drinks more alcohol than anywhere else in the world."

But the most frightening thing about this social and moral blight is that our leaders have also been involved. This is exposed in the new book, *Fit to Lead?* by Dr. Hugh Letang, editor of the London-based medical journal, *The Practitioner*. Letang documents how leaders in the last half-century have frequently made crucial decisions while drugged or drunken. For example, when Britain's Prime Minister Anthony Eden authorized the ill-conceived Suez invasion of 1956, he was taking heavy does of benzedrine, and was in "a state of acute intoxication in the technical sense of the word." The benzedrine had "created in him a hysterical paranoid obsession that Egyptian President Gamal Nasser was a new Hitler."

Letang indicates that John F. Kennedy often used pep pills and steroids, which turned him into an emotional yo-yo, bouncing between euphoria and severe depression. Using statements from Henry Kissinger, the author also discussed Richard Nixon's "drunkenness."

Letang makes a particularly frightening case out of the 1945 Yalta conference, where Churchill, Stalin, and Roosevelt re-drew the map of Europe. One eyewitness commented, "It was one of the biggest drunken brawls I ever saw." If key world leaders have made monumental decisions in the past without full control of their minds, what will happen in the future as drug use gains wider acceptance? It seems fully plausible that the nations of the world could be led into a suicidal war.

General Douglas MacArthur once warned, "We have had our last chance. The Battle of Armageddon comes next!" When I was recently in England I read a lead editorial in the *Times* which dealt with the nearness of Armageddon, identifying the place, the time, and the combatants of such a war. We do not know if this climactic conflict will include nuclear arms, but the possibility is terrifying. Pope John Paul II said in Paris that we are perilously close to the "horrible prospect of a nuclear war." The *Los Angeles Times* estimated that the U.S.A. and the U.S.S.R. have the capability to annihilate each other within about a half hour.

But will Armageddon be the end of human existence? No. Arnold Toynbee said shortly before his death, "I believe the human race will not commit suicide—it will stop just short of that." That is very close to what Jesus promised: "Except those days should be shortened, there should no flesh be saved" (Matt. 24:22). Jesus Christ will return to establish His thousand-year kingdom just before man destroys himself.

Only seven generations after Adam, Enoch prophesied:

> Behold, the Lord cometh with ten thousands of his saints, to execute judgment upon all, and to convince all that are ungodly among them of all their ungodly deeds which they have ungodly committed, and of all their hard speeches which ungodly sinners have spoken against him. (Jude 14, 15)

Jesus told His disciples, "Then shall they see the Son of man coming in a cloud with power and great glory" (Luke 21:27).

Zechariah (14:1-4) foretold a fascinating aspect of this spectacular Second Advent.

> Behold, the day of the Lord cometh. . . . For I will gather all nations against Jerusalem to battle. . . . Then shall the Lord go forth, and fight against those nations, as when he fought in the day of battle. And his feet shall stand in that day upon the mount of Olives, which is before Jerusalem on the east, and the mount of Olives shall cleave in the midst thereof toward the east and toward the west, and there shall be a very great valley; and half of the mountain shall remove toward the north, and half of it toward the south.

Revelation 16:18, 19 indicates that Christ's appearance will include "flashes of lightning, voices, peals of thunder, and a great earthquake such as had never been since men were on the earth, so great was that earthquake. The great city was split into three parts."

God told the world *over 2,000 years ago* that Jerusalem and the Mount of Olives would be ripped apart by the trauma of Christ's appearance. Seismologists are just finding out that this is possible. The Hilton Hotel corporation had wanted to build a luxury hotel on the Mount of Olives. However, a geological study revealed that the mountain is due for an earthquake of major proportions. In fact, the fissure that results will open up a waterway from the Mediterranean to the Euphrates!

The Apostle Paul assures us that Jesus will consume the Antichrist with the "brightness of his coming" (2 Thess. 2:8). And His coming will be magnificent! Let your imagination run loose as you read John's account:

> And I saw heaven open, and behold a white horse; and he that sat upon him was called Faithful and True, and in righteousness he doth judge and make war. His eyes were as a flame of fire, and on his head were many crowns; and he had a name written, that no man knew, but he himself. And he was clothed with a vesture dipped in blood: and his name is called The Word of God. And the armies which were in heaven followed him upon white horses, clothed in fine linen, white and clean. And out of his mouth goeth a sharp sword, that with it he should smite the nations: and he shall rule them with a rod of iron: and he

treadeth the winepress of the fierceness and wrath of Almighty God. And he hath on his vesture and on his thigh a name written, KING OF KINGS, AND LORD OF LORDS. And I saw the beast, and the kings of the earth, and their armies, gathered together to make war against him that sat on the horse, and against his army. And the beast was taken, and with him the false prophet that wrought miracles before him, with which he deceived them that had received the mark of the beast, and them that worshipped his image. These both were cast alive into a lake of fire burning with brimstone. (Rev. 19:11-16, 19, 20)

In the fourth century, Jerome, the Church father, forecast, "No one shall be able to assist the antichrist as the Lord vents His fury upon him. Antichrist is going to perish in that spot from which our Lord ascended to heaven." Toland's *Adolf Hitler*, a bestseller, recounts the Fuehrer's death as an ignominious, hideous burning. The demise of Antichrist will be like that, only eternal.

In early 1980, three senior rabbis in Israel reported dreams and visions of the Messiah coming to Jerusalem to subdue the peoples of the world and to establish His reign of peace and plenty. "Without the Messiah," wrote Canadian Rabbi Dr. Harvey Fields, "the human enterprise would crash into darkness forever."

Christ's triumph over Satan and his Antichrist will be the advent of the Millennium, in which Christ and His saints will rule over and renew the earth for a thousand years.

> And he laid hold on the dragon, that old serpent, which is the Devil, and Satan, and bound him a thousand years, and cast him into the bottomless pit, and shut him up, and set a seal upon him, that he should deceive the nations no more, till the thousand years should be fulfilled. . . .
>
> And I saw thrones, and they sat upon them, and judgment was given unto them: and I saw the souls of them that were beheaded for the witness of Jesus, and for the word of God, and which had not worshipped the beast, neither his image, neither had received his mark upon their foreheads, or in their hands; and they lived and reigned with Christ a thousand years. (Rev. 20:2-4)

"Everything we know," concludes Willard Libby, Nobel-Prize-winning chemist, "implies that the opportunities for future development are unbounded for a rational society operating without war." This, I believe, will be realized when Jesus Christ comes and secures His Kingdom on earth.

Throughout history, men have longed to combine compassion with competition, moral responsibility with liberty, physical labor with intellectual advance, technological development with spiritual fulfillment, liberal generosity with conservatism. This will be impossible until Christ is reigning.

The Pope was right when he admitted to a

visiting delegation that it is "not in my power to abolish war." Only Christ can do that.

One of the most beautiful prophecies concerning Christ's triumphant return was given through the prophet Micah:

> But in the last days it shall come to pass, that the mountain of the house of the Lord shall be established in the top of the mountains, and it shall be exalted above the hills; and people shall flow unto it. And many nations shall come, and say, Come, and let us go up to the mountain of the Lord, and to the house of the God of Jacob; and he will teach us of his ways, and we will walk in his paths: for the law shall go forth of Zion, and the word of the Lord from Jerusalem.
>
> And he shall judge among many people, and rebuke strong nations afar off; and they shall beat their swords into plowshares, and their spears into pruning hooks: nation shall not lift up a sword against nation, neither shall they learn war any more. (Mic. 4:1-3)

What the Church, or any other institution, has failed to do, Christ will achieve at His coming. Observes Rabbi Reuben Slonim, "Churches and synagogues have always insisted that they carried a message of supreme importance for human society. They promised to abolish war, establish the equality of all men, prohibit the exploitation of human beings, and transform the city of man into the city of God. Despite the collective of facts of all cults and creeds, the sword is still a sword, not a plowshare."

You are right, Rabbi! But Jesus, the Messiah, is coming to destroy the Antichrist and to establish His Kingdom on earth.

A recent article in *Time* stated that, while the number of the world's doctors, teachers and engineers is currently increasing very slowly, the number of military officers is rising dramatically. Christ, when He returns, will immediately reverse this trend. In fact, there will be no need for armies at all, for Jesus himself will reign. Gone will be the current annual expenditure of 600 billion dollars for armaments. Military uniforms will be collectors' items. Those 600 billion dollars will be used to subdue poverty, ignorance, and unbelief. Only then will Isaiah's ancient vision be fulfilled.

> And the government shall be upon his shoulder: and his name shall be called Wonderful, Counsellor, The mighty God, The everlasting Father, The Prince of Peace. Of the increase of his government and peace there shall be no end. (Isa. 9:6, 7)

No human negotiations or peace demonstrations can ever effect that.

The arrival of Christ as King will be the best news that a weary, exhausted, terror-ridden earth could ever hear. The beatings, the burnings, the tortures—all the pain and cruelty inflicted on people—will be banned. No more small babies with swollen bellies and discolored hair. No more terrified peasants afraid to plant rice because soldiers might come and take it away. No more hungry stomachs and slave labor camps. No more dysentery and malaria. No more sick people forced to march to their deaths. No more of Satan's evil horrors!

Dr. Alvin Silverstein, in his book *Conquest of Death,* reckons that within two decades people will be enabled by the amazing breakthroughs in medicine to lengthen life to a thousand years. Whether our Lord will use biochemical inventions or do so by celestial miracle, I do not know; but in the millennial age, where the wolf and the lamb, the lion and the cow can lie down together, man at a hundred will still be in his childhood. Money formerly squandered on missiles and bombs will buy bread for a flourishing world living under one King, with all people living in harmony as in Eden.

Every true believer is an optimistic futurist: he is looking for Jesus Christ to come and set up His Kingdom of peace and plenty, even as Peter wrote, "Nevertheless we, according to his promise, look for new heavens and a new earth, wherein dwelleth righteousness" (2 Pet. 3:13).

In his closing statement to the Global Conference on the Future, Chairman Frank Feather observed, "Some people are afraid of the future. Some want to grab it. A lot of people can't find the handle." He went on to say that man must have "transformation."

Well, Jesus Christ is the "handle" for the future! And only He can provide "transformation."

If you are looking for loopholes to justify your unbelief and disobedience to God, you're probably asking, "Isn't it possible for me to reject Jesus as Savior and Lord for the present, since I'll have an opportunity to repent and be saved during the Great Tribulation after the Church is raptured?"

My answer is an absolute "no." I believe the Gospel will be preached during those terrible times to those who have never heard. Those who have already rejected Jesus Christ will fall into the category which Paul describes in 2 Thessalonians 2:10-12:

> They received not the love of the truth, that they might be saved. And for this cause God shall send them strong delusion, that they should believe a lie [of the Antichrist]: that they all might be damned who believed not the truth, but had pleasure in unrighteousness.

If Jesus Christ is not your Lord and Savior, if you don't have the assurance of eternal life, I urge you wherever you are to bow your head and pray—honestly and earnestly—"God, be merciful to me a sinner; I wholeheartedly turn away from my sin. Save me now for Christ's sake. Cleanse me from guilt with the blood which Jesus shed on the Cross for me. Come in and take control of my life. Help me as I pray and read your Word daily to grow in grace, to become more like Jesus. Help me regularly to worship and serve you in the fellowship of your Church. I thank you for Jesus' sake. Amen."

If you have prayed that prayer, and would like spiritual counsel, I would be delighted to help you and pray for you, as well as to send you some helpful literature. Please write me today: John Wesley White, Box 1000, Milliken, Ontario, Canada.